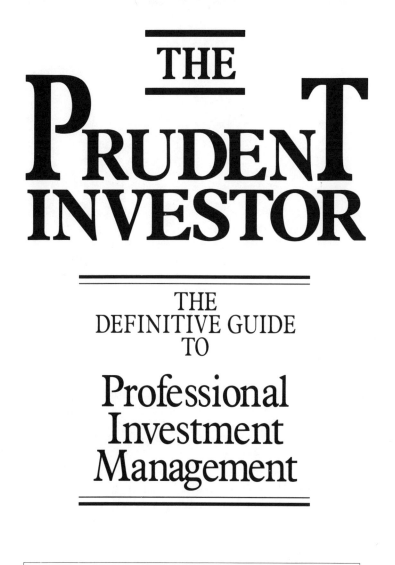

THE
PRUDENT
INVESTOR

THE DEFINITIVE GUIDE TO

Professional Investment Management

JAMES P. OWEN

PROBUS PUBLISHING COMPANY
Chicago, Illinois

This publication is designed to provide accurate and authoritative information in regard to the subject matter covered. It is sold with the understanding that the publisher is not engaged in rendering legal, accounting or other professional services.

Library of Congress Cataloging-in-Publication Data Available

ISBN: 1-55738-106-2

Cover design by Nita Alvarez

Printed in the United States of America

4   5   6   7   8   9   0

DEDICATION

To Stanya,
who came into my life 22 years ago,
and today *is* my life.

CONTENTS

ACKNOWLEDGMENTS

In addition to those quoted within the chapters, the following investment professionals contributed time, energy and insight: Richard M. Charlton, New England Pension Consultants, Inc.; Lawrence Davanzo, Wilshire Associates; Anthony R. Gray, Sun Bank Investment Management Group; Russell W. Hill, Stratford Advisory Group, Inc.; Ron Jones, Hewitt Associates; James F. Knupp, Ennis, Knupp & Associates.

Also: Dennis Larkin, Denver Investment Advisors; Matthew Lincoln, Cambridge Associates; Tony Malatino, Dean Witter Reynolds, Inc.; David O'Donovan, SEI Corp.; Bruce L. Poliquin, Avatar Associates; Richard Schilffarth, Richard Schilffarth & Associates, Ltd. and Frank Terrizzi, Renaissance Investment Management, Inc.

Further thanks go to Jeff Cohen of NWQ Investment Management Co. and Hal Rossen of Prudential-Bache Securities for their contribution to Step 10. Isabel Rosa of NWQ deserves special plaudits for her assistance and patience throughout this project.

I am indebted to the IMCA Board of Directors and Association Director Evelyn Brust for their support and encouragement.

I am grateful to Nancy Webman and Mike Clowes of *Pensions & Investments* for their editorial contributions.

Finally, this book would never have become a reality without the expertise and commitment of Robert A. Knaus and Barbara L. Darling of Vickers and Knaus.

"One thousand dollars left to earn interest at 8 percent a year will grow to $43 quadrillion in 400 years, but the first hundred years are the hardest."
SIDNEY HOMER
FROM "A HISTORY OF INTEREST RATES"

PROLOGUE

PROLOGUE:

What This Book Will Do For You

This book *is not* for the "do-it-yourself" investor or the amateur speculator. No advice is given on "how to pick this year's hottest stocks" or "how to turn $10,000 into $100,000 in six months or less."

Nor was the book written for the full-time pension officer at Xerox or the partner at Goldman, Sachs whose expertise is "international risk arbitrage."

This book *is* for the "middle-market" investor. You will benefit from reading this book if you are:

- A board member of a foundation or endowment fund.

- A trustee of a hospital or religious organization.

- A fiduciary of a public fund or Taft-Hartley plan.

- A businessman or woman who sits on a pension or profit-sharing committee.

- An attorney or CPA whose clients include "middle-market investors."

- A stockbroker or financial planner who works with high net worth individuals.

- An entrepreneur or corporate executive who has built up substantial personal assets.

3

- A small business owner responsible for his/her company's retirement plan.

- An individual who has come into a sizable inheritance.

- Anyone nearing retirement who plans to live off the income from an investment portfolio.

The goal of the book is to show you—the middle-market investor —how to take a *professional* approach to the management of your money. Specifically, you will learn: how to set investment goals and objectives; how to allocate assets among stocks, bonds, cash and alternative investments; how to select an investment manager who can best help you meet your goals and objectives; and the importance of monitoring your manager's performance so as to stay on target.

This book is not intended to be the "last word" on a wonderfully complex and ever-changing subject. Instead, we hope to give you a perspective on the correct way to look at the crucial issues, and to help you to identify the right questions to ask the professionals. By "demystifying" the process of hiring and firing money managers, this book should help you to know when you're getting sidetracked and also when you're being hoodwinked by the jargon that permeates the money management business.

And above all, it is our hope that by the time you have read through Step 10, you will have begun to truly understand a key rule of successful investing: the trade-off between risk and return.

If this book has one all-inclusive theme, however, it is summed up in the philosophy: "Get rich slowly." Anyone who has ever spent time in this field long ago lost his or her illusion that somewhere out there is a money manager who "walks on water," or has the "keys to the kingdom" and who can actually speed up the investment process and, in effect, make you rich overnight.

Indeed, we feel the most important characteristic that sets truly successful investors apart from the crowd is *patience*, the willingness to take a long-term view. When you put time on your side, and begin to understand what Einstein once labeled the greatest force in the universe—the power of compound interest—you begin to put that power to work in your portfolio.

A successful businessperson, someone who manufactures a product, for example, might argue that if you work hard enough or apply enough energy or brainpower to any problem, you can quickly overcome it. That's simply not true of the investment process. In fact, sometimes you can try too hard, and you find that all of the thrashing around, all the urgency to make things happen is counterproductive; successful investing requires giving something time to work out.

A corollary to this truth is the importance that *consistency* plays in the performance of a money manager. And here the proverbial fable of the tortoise and the hare provides a very apt analogy: Do you hire the "hot" manager who touts spectacular short-term performance or the more conservative manager who turns in less spectacular, but consistently good numbers, quarter after quarter, year after year. Experience has shown that it is the latter, not the former, who ends up winning the race.

If, as a middle-market investor, you can truly come to understand this concept and put it to work in your portfolio, you will have taken a giant step toward maximizing the performance of your investment portfolio.

Slowly. Consistently. And very, very successfully.

James P. Owen
Vail, Colorado

STEP 1

STEP 1:

Taking Stock

"I've got all the money I'll ever
need if I die by four o'clock."
HENNY YOUNGMAN

Although this book was created to improve the performance of your portfolio, you really can't do that without first taking stock. That is, before you step forward, you must look backward. This will give you a fresh perspective on where you are now, and, more importantly, how you got there.

This first step isn't nearly as difficult as you might imagine. Start by writing a simple, one- to two-page narrative of the history of your fund. Make it as personal and anecdotal as you can. If you are the trustee of a pension or endowment fund, for example, it might go something like this:

> *"When we started, our portfolio was fairly small, and since the chairman of our investment committee had made some money in the stock market himself, we pretty much let him call the shots. Things went reasonably well, until the 1973-74 bear market, when we took a real bath in some high fliers. So much for managing the money internally.*
>
> *"One of our board members was chairman of the local bank, so it seemed natural to turn our account over to its trust department. Five years later, because of bad performance, we fired them. But in all fairness, the bank wasn't totally to blame; the*

9

only guidance we had given them was: 'Do the best job you can for us.' The final straw was the high turnover of trust officers assigned to our portfolio. We seemed to get a new one every six months; not one could have been over 30.

"We then went with an insurance company, which convinced us the best way to lock in high current yields was to buy something called guaranteed investment contracts. What they didn't tell us was that GICs were virtually illiquid, and the next thing we knew, we were stuck earning fixed returns while interest rates went through the roof!

"Finally, the happy experience of one of our directors led us to an old line Boston counseling firm. Because of our earlier disaster with speculative stocks, we instructed them to divide our portfolio between conservative blue-chip issues—like IBM—and long-term, investment-grade bonds. The firm gave us excellent service, and we'd probably still be with them had our attorney not advised us that, as fiduciaries, we'd be prudent to hire an independent consultant to monitor our manager's performance.

"The consultant's findings shocked us! Compared to similar funds, we never ranked above the median manager in any of the five years we were with the manager, and, on a cumulative basis, we ranked in the bottom one-third of the consultant's data base. Moreover, we'd only managed to beat the market in one out of the five years.

"The consultant has recommended we drop our balanced manager and diversify among a whole host of specialized equity and fixed-income managers, each with a label more exotic-sounding than the next. Frankly, we're more confused than ever, and are not sure what to do at this point."

Or, if you are a high net worth individual —perhaps someone who recently sold your own company—your narrative might sound something like this:

While I took high risks to build my business, I know one thing for sure: I'm unwilling to take those kinds of risks again. I want my assets to grow, but if I lose this money, I'm too old to start over. Besides, I want to relax and have some fun now.

"And while I did a good job creating wealth, I'm not sure I have the expertise to manage it. I know I need professional help, but I worry about turning over control of my assets to someone else. After all, I built my company by making all the decisions myself.

"I'm not lacking for advice. Financial planners, stockbrokers, personal bankers, even my CPA, my attorney and my insurance agent all seem to be trying to sell me something. Frankly, I'm getting a little bit cynical. Where do I find truly objective advice?"

Does any of this sound familiar? We've asked you to go through this exercise for two reasons. First, a "financial disrobing" should uncover a whole set of biases—what you like and dislike about the financial markets, investment professionals and so on. These biases are very important—more important than most people realize—in determining your comfort level with different asset classes and your attitude toward investment risk.

Indeed, we probably can make the following assumptions about the biases of the investors in the two narratives:

- The committee probably won't deliver its assets into the hands of bankers anytime soon.

- Likewise, GICs and junior portfolio managers are in disfavor as are firms with a lot of personnel turnover.

- The committee most likely will take a somewhat jaundiced view of balanced management in general and bonds with long maturities in particular.

- The entrepreneur clearly has a bias against turning over control of his assets to professionals; he worries about conflicts of interest and doesn't trust others to make decisions for him.

Right or wrong, such biases must be recognized, examined and dealt with before you can take the next step toward maximizing the returns on your portfolio.

The second reason we asked you to do this stocktaking exercise is that you can learn valuable lessons from your past mistakes. When committee members in the above narrative, for example, turned their chairman loose to buy highly speculative stocks, they discovered the importance of determining how much risk they'd be willing to incur *before* embarking on an investment program. They also learned they shouldn't take such a passive role in the management of their fund, and should become *actively* involved in both the manager hiring decisions and the continuous monitoring of performance.

While the entrepreneur hasn't made a mistake yet, he could be about to—by choosing to manage his own money. He might discover the risk-taking mentality that built his fortune could quickly wipe him out in the financial markets.

Perhaps the biggest mistake many middle-market investors make, however, is to assume the only way to maximize performance is through dramatic increases in annual returns. This is simply not true. Ask any professional: Such increases are all but impossible to sustain because this year's "hot" money manager more than likely will be next year's big loser.

And more importantly, every big reward carries with it an equally big risk. The *real* key to improved long-term performance rests in small incremental gains driven by that most wonderful of financial marvels—the power of compounding.

The following table, for example, shows what a $1 million fund would earn by increasing its return from 10% to 12% to 15% over five, 10 and 15 years. As you can see, over the long haul, small consistent gains can multiply into very big gains!

HOW $1 MILLION MULTIPLIES

	10%	*12%*	*15%*
5 years	$1,610,510	$1,762,341	$2,011,357
10 years	$2,593,742	$3,105,848	$4,045,558
15 years	$4,177,248	$5,473,566	$8,137,062

How do you achieve these incremental increases? The real secret is so simple, and seemingly obvious, that many investors miss it:

Don't focus on trying to beat the market or trying to beat other investors, which you can't control; instead, emphasize the avoidance of mistakes, which you *can* control.

That is the clear message of this book. By identifying the common mistakes made by other middle-market investors, we hope to help you avoid those mistakes and by so doing, to dramatically increase your chances of achieving higher investment returns.

Now that you've taken stock of how you got to where you are today, you're ready to move on. The next step (Step 2) will help you set the target rates of return and acceptable risk levels that serve as the foundation of your investment policy. Once you know what you want to accomplish, you can choose the proper asset allocation to get you there (Step 3). With your money divided among various capital markets, you'll have to decide what investment styles you're comfortable with (Step 4) and learn how to choose investment managers who can best help you reach your goals (Step 5). Next, you'll want to make sure you're staying on target (Step 6) and know when your money manager is in trouble (Step 7). And should you decide to venture beyond stocks and bonds, you'll need some understanding of alternative investments (Step 8). Then, you'll learn how investment management consultants can help you put all the steps together (Step 9) and, finally, with our glossary of terms at your side (Step 10), you'll be able to decipher "investment-speak."

Having reached this point, you've already completed Step 1. And everybody knows the toughest part of any journey is taking the first step.

STEP 2

STEP 2:

Looking Forward: The Investment Policy Statement

"The safest way to double your money is to fold it over once and put it in your pocket."
FRANK MCKINNEY HUBBARD

Once you know where you are, the first step in a professional approach to managing your assets is to develop an *investment policy statement,* which defines where you want to go and how you want to get there.

Imagine the investment policy statement as an investor's version of a flight plan for a pilot flying between New York and Los Angeles. Without the flight plan, the pilot would get in his plane in New York without any knowledge of how to get to LA. The possible mishaps are frightening: He could run out of fuel without knowing the most direct route; he could encounter turbulent weather; he could collide with other aircraft because he's off course; or he could fly out into the Atlantic rather than west across the country.

Mishaps of the same proportions could befall the middle-market investor who isn't guided by any policy.

An investment policy statement is a *written statement* of the *goals* for the portfolio and the *rules* to be followed by money managers to achieve those goals. It establishes a target rate of return, guidelines for the amount of risk managers may accept in pursuit of the target and any other restrictions by which managers must abide.

17

This chapter will first explain some common problems you might encounter, then will discuss the important elements—the investment objective or target; the level of risk that is acceptable; and special rules, guidelines and/or restrictions—and, finally, will show you how to put everything together.

Once you've set your policy and established your risk and return objectives, it will serve as the framework for allocating the assets among various investment classes, hiring investment managers, and monitoring performance (each of which is covered in separate chapters). It also guides the managers in their investment activities.

In short, this chapter will explain how to get through the most important, but also the most tedious and time-consuming, process you will endure. You will learn how to write a document that can help to assure the success of your investment program more so than any other steps you take; that document is the investment policy statement. First, though, we will explore three common pitfalls associated with this most crucial step.

Mistake #1:   No investment policy statement.

The single biggest and most common mistake middle-market investors make is they simply don't have an investment policy statement. In fact, many defined benefit plans, foundations, endowments and wealthy individuals invest almost arbitrarily. The folly of arbitrary investing in a defined benefit (or pension) plan is readily apparent: Since a sponsor guarantees a benefit to retirees, investment actions taken to meet that guarantee must be made as deliberately as possible; otherwise, the sponsor will have to make up the shortfall between the money promised and the money available for meeting that promise.

But the problem could be even more common in defined contribution plans. Sponsors of defined contribution plans might think they can operate their plans without investment policies because the company won't have to make up any shortfall from poor investment decisions. Still, written objectives are necessary, even in defined contribution plans, because they prove the employer has made every effort to choose the right investment vehicles and the right investment managers. A badly managed defined contribution plan could get the sponsor sued by disgruntled retirees.

Mistake #2: The investment policy statement is unrealistic, ill-defined, or contradictory.

One major consulting firm conducted a survey of middle-market investors, asking them if they had investment policies and, if so, what the policies stated. The majority said they did have such policies, but when asked to elaborate, far too many of them stated their policies as: "The money manager has full discretion." Giving the manager control over all of the investment decisions is not a policy; it is a way of abdicating responsibility for formulating that policy.

Writing the policy involves making hard choices. If your manager fails to perform, would you rather lose money in a bear market or underperform in a bull market? Faced with that choice, which would you pick? It is unrealistic to say: "When the market's up, we want to be in it; when it's down, we want to be out." Realistically, if an investor or money manager was prophetic enough to know precisely when the market would move up or down, he or she wouldn't have to work for a living.

The October 1987 stock market crash helped tame some investors' unrealistic expectations. Until then, many investors would say they were risk averse but wanted a 20% return. They didn't understand the trade-off between risk and reward—the greater the reward, the greater the risk. Even since the crash, when investors say they want moderate risk and want to preserve capital, they're still hopeful of seeing 15% rates of return with low exposure to stocks, the asset class that has had the highest returns over the long term.

Many middle-market investors have vague investment policies that state the obvious without giving managers any genuine guidance. Statements such as "little or no risk," or "maximize return," or "preserve capital" are virtually useless to a portfolio manager unless they are defined and explained by you. Your definition and your manager's definition must match, or each of you will have different expectations and someone is likely to be disappointed.

Investment managers can add to the problem. Every investor knows of at least one manager who, in the course of trying to win his/her business, has said, "Trust me. Not only will I outperform other managers and the S&P 500 (Standard & Poor's 500 stock index) when the market's hot, I'll get you out of stocks altogether when the market is going down." Remember, if it sounds too good to be true, it probably is.

Mistake #3:   The investment policy statement is ignored.

Even if you have a realistic investment policy statement, you're not home free. That's because there's a good chance that the investment policy statement is ignored. "Organizations that have policy statements rarely follow them," laments Dave Kudish, head of Stratford Advisory Group, Inc., an investment management consulting firm. "The statement is like a fire extinguisher: The code says you have to have one, but you don't have to use it."

The importance of the policy statement can't be overstated. Trustees must ask: "Where are we going with this fund? What do we want to accomplish?"

In defined benefit funds, for which the most detailed policies usually are written, the policy becomes the "fingerprint of the fiscal health of the plan," believes Roger Bransford, national director of asset consulting for TPF&C, a consulting firm. The fiscal health includes its funded status, or the amount of assets available to pay liabilities; liquidity, availability of money to pay benefits when due; the level of plan contributions, usually expressed as a percentage of payroll; and the expense component, or how the plan expenses affect the sponsor's bottom line.

Even for defined contribution plans, where there is no firm promise to pay benefits, there is still an implied promise that requires an assessment of fiscal health. In addition, trustees of defined contribution plans must decide whether they are providing a savings vehicle or a retirement vehicle, then set policy accordingly, and develop a strategy for each investment option in the plan.

Now, let's walk through the stages to setting investment policy so you can see that while the process is lengthy, it is manageable.

Stage 1:   Deciding when to set policy.

Investors need to formulate or reformulate their policy in some period of calm, rather than in a crisis. Many investment consultants and managers tell of trustees deciding to flee the stock market following 1987's stock market meltdown. They scrambled to revamp investment policies and terminate money managers. In the process, many turned what should have been a deliberate, thoughtful and systematic process into a knee-jerk reaction to an event. One year later, when the market rose sharply (as illustrated on page 22), these same trustees probably felt remorse.

Stage 2:   Determining who sets the policy.

Only the asset owner—the sponsor of the plan—can make the investment policy decision. The sponsor might need help from actuarial and investment management consultants, but the responsibility still rests with the sponsor.

Even when plan sponsors accept responsibility for making the decision, they still might take the easy way out by emulating someone else's investment policy. The chairman of Company A might like the way the chairman of Company B runs his company, so he emulates Company B's investment policy. But what is appropriate for one company and its plan or for one endowment/foundation, might not be appropriate for another.

Stage 3:   Understanding the characteristics of the policy and the tests it must withstand.

Your investment policy must be long term in nature; it must be separate from the portfolio management structure (because the policy shapes the investments, rather than the investments shaping

RECOVERY FROM THE "CRASH" OF 1987

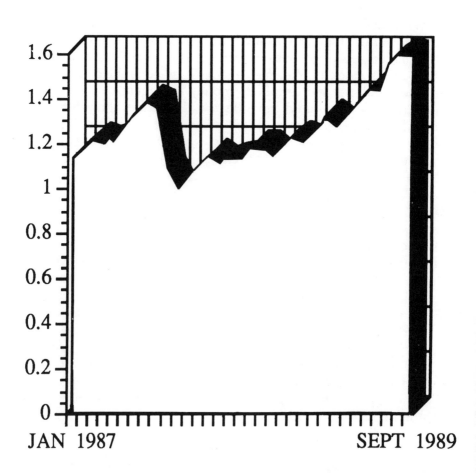

Growth of the S&P 500

Source: SEI Corporation

the policy), so it can't have a market or economic point of view; and it must be responsive to the need for which the assets exist. In the case of a defined benefit plan, the need would be to pay liabilities; in the case of an endowment, to fund programs; in the case of an individual, to retire comfortably and securely at a certain age.

In formulating the policy, make sure it is explicit enough that an investment manager (or in industry jargon, a "competent stranger") could carry out your instructions in the course of managing your assets. The manager has to be able to read your policy and say, "I really understand what you're trying to accomplish." If not, you—the investor—will be disappointed, and it could take you even longer to achieve your goals if you have to change course or change investment managers in midstream.

To test whether it is exclusive of market and economic considerations, ask yourself whether the policy could have been followed in the past 10 or more years; that is, make sure it would have withstood the prevailing capital market conditions. Ask yourself, "What would have happened if my managers had followed it to the letter? Would my investments have produced acceptable results?"

Consultant Charles Ellis, who considers investment policy crucial enough that he wrote an entire book on it, lists six questions (which we've expanded on) to think through before writing the policy statement.[1]

- What are the real risks of an adverse outcome? Define an adverse outcome (underperforming the market, or your target rate of return, or producing a negative return), then define the risks (increased contributions, which, for a corporation, decrease the amount of available capital to spend in other areas; an unfunded liability, meaning there isn't enough in assets to pay vested benefits; or maybe you'll lose your position as a trustee).

- What are your probable emotional reactions to an adverse outcome? Perhaps you'll panic, deciding to radically change

---

1   Charles D. Ellis, *Investment Policy*, (Homewood, Illinois: Dow Jones-Irwin, 1985).

the investment policy to ensure fewer sleepless nights, or you could assume you'll handle the news calmly, and might simply reexamine the investment policy to determine if it is sound.

- How knowledgeable are you about investments and markets?

- What other capital or income resources does the plan sponsor have and how important is this portfolio to its overall financial position? For example, if this is a defined contribution plan that is supplementing a defined benefit plan, the plan might not be as important to the sponsor as it would be if it were the only retirement plan. Of course, participants tend to treat a defined contribution plan as life or death. A defined benefit plan, on the other hand, could be considered a source of capital within the overall financial structure of the company; the chief financial officer might assume that if the plan becomes too overfunded, the company will terminate it to put the excess assets into the corporate coffers.

- Are there any legal restrictions that will be imposed on the investment policy (such as a prohibition against investing in equities or a requirement to make so-called social investments)?

- Are there any unanticipated consequences of interim fluctuations in portfolio value that might affect policy? If you're paying out much more in benefits than you're taking in through contributions, you might want your portfolio to be invested in such a way that at least a good portion of it doesn't fluctuate in value, that it provides a steady income stream.

Stage 4: Developing the financial profile of the fund and its sponsor.

The stage of growth of both must be determined. If the assets are in a corporate defined benefit plan, for example, you must figure out whether both the fund and the company (the plan sponsor) are in the start-up, early growth, later growth, mature or declining stage. A young, growing company likely has a young work force. A defined benefit plan for younger workers can set a higher rate of return objective and can tolerate more risk than can a mature company with many plan participants at or near retirement. That's because the plan assets of the younger company (with the younger work force) don't need to be as liquid since there will be fewer retirees to whom to pay benefits. The fund and its sponsor also are in a better position to suffer some subpar investment performance because they will have time to make up for the unrewarded risk before the money will be needed to pay benefits.

For the younger company with a defined benefit plan, incurring more risk to reach a higher rate of return objective will save the company money, if successful. A percentage point increase in annual return will reduce the cost of funding the plan by 15% to 20%, many investment professionals agree.

A company with a mature plan, however, can't take that kind of risk. If its investments aren't successful, the company still will have to meet high benefit payments and will have to amortize the losses if the actual investment results are lower than the plan's actuarial investment assumption.

Linking assets to liabilities is of paramount importance in a defined benefit plan. On the liability side, trustees must know the estimated growth in the work force, and project inflation and the cost of benefits over the next 20 to 30 years, before they can determine how best to invest the assets.

Although pension plans take into account future contributions, trustees and executives of foundations and endowments typically can't count on any source of new revenue except investment returns. The head of one of the nation's largest foundations learned that lesson the hard way when he moved to the foundation from a big corporate pension fund. Shortly after he arrived he asked his boss: "When do I get my next contribution?" The reply, "What you see is what you get," illustrates a major difference between pension plans and foundations. Endowments often have some irregular cash flow from alumni or donors, but it can't be counted on.

Just as pension plans link assets and liabilities, foundations and endowments link assets and the spending or distribution rate. The investment program should create a stream of revenues that will grow at least as fast as inflation. That means the spending rate plus inflation must equal the targeted rate of return. Trustees of foundations and endowments, therefore, must understand that the more money they want to spend, the more they'll have to invest in riskier investments that have the potential for greater long-term returns (but also for poorer results short term). Generally, their rate of return objectives are high: Many are required or need to spend 5% of their assets on programs, which means they will have to earn a 5% return on investments over inflation just to stay even. Those who insist on spending 7% or even 10% of the fund's assets must accept the fact that they likely will have to erode or invade principal. That's a bitter pill for most trustees to swallow.

The financial health of the plan sponsor and the plan also is an important consideration.

A company with cyclical (or, worse, weak) earnings and a debt-ridden balance sheet can ill afford to allow its pension fund to take risks. A company with strong earnings and a healthy balance sheet, on the other hand, could ante up more money to fund the plan, if necessary.

Similarly, a different set of investment objectives would be fashioned for a fund that has an unfunded liability (meaning it has less in assets than would be needed to pay benefits) than for a fund that is overfunded (meaning it has more in assets than would be needed to pay benefits).

Stage 5: Assessing the needs of the fund.

Now begins the nitty-gritty work of setting the investment objectives. The first step is to establish what amount of investment return the fund needs. In the case of a defined benefit plan, for example, the plan's actuary will devise an interest rate (or rate of return) assumption that should be a starting point for you. The actuarial interest assumption is the actuary's best estimate of the long-term rate of return the fund must earn on its investment. The actuary uses this interest-rate assumption to calculate the present value of the long-term liabilities of the fund and, thus, how much the sponsor must contribute each year. But the interest assumption is very conservative. A higher target is needed so the fund will have a cushion—to allow for contingencies in the plan or in the sponsoring company itself. The fund's specific needs will determine the final rate of return objective.

Here's where you take into account the characteristics of the participants in the plan—if it is an employee benefit fund—such as average age and length of service and percentage of active vs. retired participants. Defined contribution plans also must contend with employee turnover rates and withdrawal provisions when determining liquidity requirements.

Also consider the characteristics of the plan itself. As we explained, trustees of endowments and foundations must know how much of the fund they want to distribute each year, and will set a return objective consistent with depleting none or only a small percentage of the principal.

Trustees of defined contribution plans might consider safety of principal to be of utmost importance. That's because retirement income in a defined contribution plan depends only on contributions and investment success, rather than on any guarantee of specific benefits paid to retirees. Defined contribution plans are likely to take fewer risks (and therefore have lower return expectations) than their defined benefit counterparts. Plus, trustees of defined contribution plans have to present their results to the participants each year, and participants aren't going to be happy with losses, since it is their money and not the company's money that's at stake.

But some pension fund executives contend that if their company's defined contribution plan supplements a defined benefit plan, it can be invested more aggressively than the defined benefit plan because retirees won't be counting on it to provide their major retirement benefits.

Stage 6: Dealing with return.

Once the needs are assessed, the key then is to set risk and return objectives, which form the heart of your investment policy statement. Never mind that volumes of books have been written on just these two elements. We'll give you the basics, beginning with rate of return, then explaining risk and, finally, discussing the relationship between the two.

We've already explained the way it works for foundations and endowments; that is, the return must, at least, equal spending plus inflation, also known as the real rate of return. But for employee benefit funds, especially for defined benefit plans, the process is more intricate because of the needs of the plan and of the sponsor.

When you're talking about return, you must determine whether you are more interested in a *relative rate of return* (how you performed compared to everyone else or to a proxy for the market, such as the Standard & Poor's 500 stock index) or an *absolute rate of return* (just how much money you actually earned or lost).

Many investors claim they are relative-oriented, but they aren't. "Almost everyone is relative-oriented in a bull market and absolute-oriented in a bear market," says Charles C. Field, vice president of the money management firm Lowe, Brockenbrough, Tierney & Tattersall. In a bull market, they want their return to be as close as possible to the top returns or, at least, to a benchmark like the S&P 500. In a bear market, they don't care how anyone else fared as long as they didn't lose money.

Field uses this example to make his point to trustees: "If I'm your manager and I walk into your office and say, 'I have good news and bad news. The good news is your fund ranks in the top 10 percent of funds in the country; the bad news is you were down 18%,' how would you react?" According to Field, most investors will raise the roof because they lost 18%. That shows they are less interested in how their assets performed relative to the market than they are in the absolute rate of return their assets earned, at least in a bear market.

Conversely, Field notes, many balanced money managers (those who invest in stocks, bonds and cash) and defensive managers (those who give up some return in an up market to ensure they're protected in a down market) had a tough time drawing interest during the raging bull market that preceded 1987's meltdown. At that time, he remembers, investors were interested only in relative returns. He recalls hearing such comments as: "Why do I want to talk to you when you had an 18% (annualized) return and the guy I just talked to had a 30% (annualized) return over the last three years?" The investor, impressed by the high-flying manager's bull-market performance, never questioned how much of a beating that manager might take in a down market.

Noel Feldman, a partner in Hewitt Associates, contends trustees are "fighting the last investment battle" by focusing on recent capital markets history, rather than their future needs, when they set return objectives. In the mid-1970s, he remembers, investment policies were written with absolute target returns, but when inflation reached double digits, policies were rewritten to express inflation-related return objectives. With inflation now a fraction of what it used to be, Feldman asserts, beating inflation is no longer a major accomplishment. "A forward-thinking trustee today would say, 'I can't believe we've had such good returns, and, since the plan is overfunded, let's see what absolute return we need and let's shoot for that.' I haven't talked to any plans that have had the courage to do that," Feldman says.

One way to determine the rate of return objective of a defined benefit plan is in relation to the real return required to balance the funding of the plan.

Duncan Smith, senior vice president-manager of research for Frank Russell Co., suggests obtaining from your fund's actuary the level of future inflation incorporated into the funding calculations as well as the actuarial assumptions for salary and investment return.[2] If the actuary provides the inflation estimate, Smith says, you would need only to know the investment return assumption to identify the required real return (that which is in excess of inflation). In that case, the inflation assumption is subtracted from the investment return assumption; the remainder is the required real rate of return.

Alternately, the regular annual evaluation report from the actuary will include—usually in the appendix—the investment and

---

2   Duncan Smith, *How to Select and Evaluate Investment Managers*, (Tacoma, Washington: Frank Russell Co. 1988).

salary assumptions. Using these, Smith says, you can perform the following calculation:

	Actuarial investment return assumption	8.%
(minus)	Actuarial salary increase assumption	-6.0%
(equals)	Funding policy spread	2.00%
(plus)	Estimated career real wage gain	+1.5%
(equals)	Required real return to balance funding	3.5%

But Smith's method doesn't tell us anything about what history has taught us about returns, which is something every investor needs to study.

Investment management scholars and practitioners Roger Ibbotson and Rex Sinquefield traced historical rates of return for the 63-year period between 1926 and 1988 and updated in 1989.[3] (See pages 31 and 32.) They found the average return on common stocks was 10%; long-term corporate bonds, 5%; long-term government bonds, 4.4%; and U.S. Treasury bills, 3.5%. Real rates of return (returns above inflation) were 6.7% for common stocks; 1.9% for long-term corporate bonds; 1.2% for long-term government bonds; and 0.5% for Treasury bills.

What does this tell us about what kind of returns are reasonable to expect in the future? Nothing absolute, because there's no guarantee the next 63 years will resemble the previous 63. Indeed, there is debate about just how far back into history investors should look. David T. Ferrier, vice president of the consulting services division of Merrill Lynch, points out that the past 10 years produced far higher annual returns than the 50 before them. And on the bond side, he notes, returns since the 1940s indicate investors would have been better off in intermediate-term bonds than in long-term ones. "But you can't assume intermediate-term bonds will outperform long-term bonds in the future," he says.

Robert Marchesi, president of DeMarche Associates consultants, said the Ibbotson/Sinquefield returns are not necessarily reliable for

---

3   Roger G. Ibbotson and Rex A. Sinquefield, *Stocks, Bonds, Bills and Inflation 1982*, updated in 1989 Yearbook, Ibbotson Associates Inc., Chicago. All rights reserved.

SUMMARY STATISTICS OF ANNUAL RETURNS (1926–1988)

Series	Geometric Mean	Arithmetic Mean	Standard Deviation	Distribution
Common Stocks	10.0%	12.1%	20.9%	
Small Company Stocks	12.3	17.8	35.6	
Long-Term Corporate Bonds	5.0	5.3	8.4	
Long-Term Government Bonds	4.4	4.7	8.5	
Intermediate-Term Government Bonds	4.8	4.9	5.5	
U.S. Treasury Bills	3.5	3.6	3.3	
Inflation Rates	3.1	3.2	4.8	

-90% 0% 90%

Source: Ibbotson Associates

WEALTH INDICES OF INVESTMENTS IN THE
U.S. CAPITAL MARKETS (1926–1988)

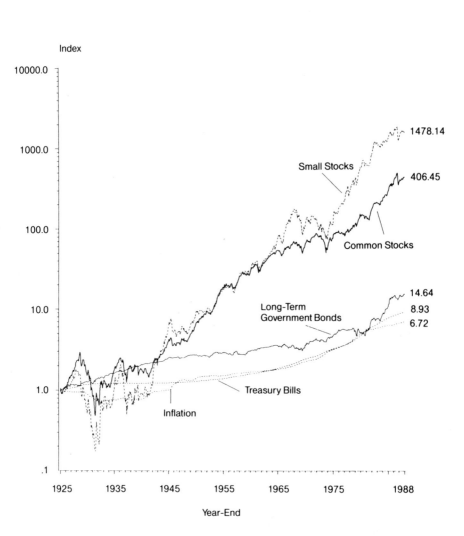

Source: Ibbotson Associates

looking forward. Bond returns, for example, are driven by the level of inflation, meaning high inflation brings high bond rates. According to Marchesi, most of the Ibbotson/Sinquefield data came from years of low inflation, so that's why bond returns were low.

Still, when risk (variability or volatility of returns) is factored in, these statistics do lend credence to the notion that risk is rewarded over the long term. Stocks, the most risky investment Ibbotson and Sinquefield tracked, had the highest return, while Treasury bills, the least risky, had the lowest return. And Marchesi still believes stocks will outperform bonds and Treasury bills (also known as cash or cash equivalents) over the long term.

Interviews with plan sponsors, consultants and investment managers provide a glimpse of real rates of return (returns above inflation) they consider reasonable these days: 5%-7% for stocks; 3%-4% for bonds; 1%-2% for cash; 7%-10% for international securities; and 5%-6% for real estate.

When establishing a target return, be aware that the average rate of return has three main components: the risk-free rate of return; a premium over that rate that offsets the effect of inflation on your purchasing power; and a premium over the inflation-adjusted risk-free rate of return to compensate for market risk.

Stage 7: Understanding risk.

Now that risk has been introduced, let's deal with it. First, understand that risk drives returns, rather than the other way around. Second, become familiar with what risk means and what kinds of risk exist.

When you're talking to money managers or investment management consultants, they often will refer to risk, in its basic form, as the level of uncertainty about the returns expected from an investment. Thus, risk is defined as volatility, or the frequency and amount a certain investment fluctuates (or deviates) from its average return. The more the investment deviates from that return, the more volatile and, hence, risky, it is, even if the investment often produces higher-than-average returns. As an example, imagine that stock A has an annual return of 10% over 10 years, but its return has been as high as 20% some years and as low as zero in other years. Stock B, on the other hand, has an 8% annual return, with a high of 15% in some years and a low of 5% in other years. Which stock has been less risky? Stock B.

The point is, you can't depend on that investment to behave predictably. If it produced unpredictably high returns during the past 10 years, it's volatile enough to produce unpredictably low returns in the future.

Volatility, or risk, can be measured through standard deviation, or the range of price fluctuations likely for a particular investment. Statistically, standard deviation is a measure of the extent to which observations of a security's price behavior differ from the arithmetic mean. Studies measuring standard deviation have shown that stocks are more likely to deviate from an average return than are bonds, and that's why stocks are thought to be more risky than bonds. For example, stocks have a long-term average return of 10% and a standard deviation of 20.9% in the Ibbotson/Sinquefield study. That is, the return in any year could range from 10% *plus* 20.9% or 10% *minus* 20.9%. For long-term corporate bonds, the average return is 5%, and the standard deviation is only 8.4%.

"As you increase return, you increase risk. You just can't have your cake and eat it too," says DeMarche's Marchesi.

This measurement of risk is by no means perfect, largely because it deals with the past: Volatility can't be determined until the return is known, so you can only hope the asset class will behave the same in the future (in regard to variability or standard deviation) as it has in the past.

But when they talk about investment risk, managers and consultants are also referring to market risk. Market risk is the volatility in a stock's price caused by movements in the market as a whole. When the market crashed on Oct. 19, 1987, no stock was immune. Every stock, no matter how good the company, felt the impact. Yet different stocks fell different amounts. Some fell more than the market indexes, and some less. Thus, some were less risky than others. Similarly, the market moves all airline stocks the same way. But the strike at Eastern Airlines in 1989 caused the price of Eastern's stock to move more, overwhelming the effects of market risk.

Market risk, which can't be avoided, is estimated by calculating the historical price behavior of a security on a weighted average, then relating that to changes in the market as a whole. Part of what you're doing when you set your investment policy is deciding what level of market risk you are willing to accept. Then, when you hire a money manager and ask him/her to agree to your policy statement, the manager is agreeing to manage that market risk.

One way to quantify the riskiness of a particular stock is by determining its beta. Starting with the assumption that the Standard & Poor's 500 stock index has a beta of one, a stock with a beta of one, then, moves with the S&P 500. A stock with a beta of 1.4, for example, will rise and fall 40% more than the S&P 500 will and a stock with a beta of 0.6% will go up and down 60% as much as the S&P 500. Some investment policy statements are so specific they give money managers guidelines on beta, such as instructions to purchase only those stocks with a beta of between 0.8% and 1.2%.

Failing to quantify risk is one of the most common mistakes an investor can make. An investment policy statement that says, "We'd like a return in excess of the S&P 500," is useless unless the investor states what risks he/she is willing to take to achieve that goal.

The risks found in individual and groups of stocks can be largely avoided by constructing a portfolio that replicates the market, such as an index fund.

And just as you reduce risk by owning a diversified number of stocks, you can reduce systematic risk—the risk of owning an entire class of securities—by diversifying among asset classes, such as by investing not just in stocks and bonds, but also by allocating assets to other investment classes such as real estate.

When you spread the risk by investing in more than one asset class, another investment term—covariance—must be dealt with. Covariance measures the correlation of a pair of assets, revealing the degree to which their returns are related. Perfectly correlated assets have correlation coefficients of +1, meaning the expected returns of each of the pair of assets will move in the same direction by proportionately the same amount. The lower the correlation, the more likely you can improve returns without adding more risk. Real estate sometimes is added to a portfolio because it is the only asset category that generally is inversely related to bonds and is unrelated to stocks in the short run.

For some investors, however, volatility is not the sole, or even most important, risk that exists in investing. What about, for example, the low beta stock that suddenly is hammered by a totally unpredictable disaster that befalls the company? This can't be quantified, but you need to be aware of the possibility just as you need to be aware of the possibility that you can have a serious accident while driving a car. There's also the view that the short-term volatility or swings in the price of a stock are of relative unimportance to a supposedly long-term investor like a pension fund.

You might put risk in a different light. You might ask yourself: "Do I have to have a positive return each year? If not, what about a 5% loss? A 10% loss?" You also might define risk as the amount of money you think you could lose and still sleep through the night. Or, you might wonder how far down your portfolio would have to drop in a bear market before you literally said, "I wish to God I'd never heard of my money manager."

Research conducted by Salomon Brothers, Inc. could prompt trustees and investment professionals to think about risk in still another way. In a report published in January 1989, Salomon's Martin L. Leibowitz and Terence C. Langetieg discussed "shortfall risk," the probability that one of your goals—such as achieving your target rate of return or preserving the surplus that exists in your fund—could be jeopardized.[4]

Using the widely accepted historical return data compiled by Ibbotson Associates and the standard volatility assumptions we discussed above, the two researchers found equity risk is more "stubbornly persistent" than is commonly believed. Specifically, they said there's a 36% chance that stocks will underperform bonds in any five-year period and a 24% chance stocks will underperform bonds in any 20-year period. (Of course, that also means that in any 20-year period, there is a 76% chance stocks will outperform bonds.)

---

4   Martin L. Leibowitz and Terence C. Langetieg, *Shortfall Risks and the Asset Allocation Decision*, (New York: Salomon Brothers Inc., January 1989).

Here's an example to illustrate how their revelations about equity risk can affect your objectives: Imagine you oversee a $10.25 million pension plan that has surplus assets (that is, assets in excess of what's needed to pay vested benefits) of $2.5 million and a funding ratio (how fully funded the plan is) of 125%. Your goals are to achieve a minimum rate of return of 9% and to produce enough of a return that you don't have to report a deficit.

Using the standard return and risk assumptions and a five-year time horizon, they conclude that an allocation of 30% stocks and 70% bonds results in a higher probability that you will meet your goals than does any other allocation they studied. Indeed, they found with the 30/70 stock and bond allocation, there is a 33% chance you won't achieve a minimum return of 9% and an 8% chance you'll have a deficit. With 60% allocated to stocks and 40% to bonds, however, there is a 34% chance you won't hit the target return and a 14% chance you'll have a deficit. At 100% bonds, on the other hand, there's a 50% chance you won't hit the 9% return and a 9% chance you'll suffer a deficit.

THREE EXAMPLES OF SHORTFALL RISK

Asset mix stocks/bonds	Chance of missing goal	Chance of deficit
60%/40%	34%	14%
30%/70%	33%	8%
0/100%	50%	9%

Stock allocations above 30%, Leibowitz and Langetieg found, produce greater shortfall risk measured either in terms of the rate of return objective or the probability of a deficit. "To justify a stock allocation higher than 30%," they said, "one must carefully weight the incremental rewards against the incremental risks of jeopardizing strategic objectives."

Those who provide asset and liability modeling and forecasting services believe a new definition of risk or volatility is warranted. They define risk as the volatility of pension contributions and pension expense and the degree of underfunding. This is particularly important to corporations in light of the Financial Accounting Standards Board's requirements to include pension expense on their balance sheets, known as FASB Statement 87. Corporations now must recognize changes in the funding status—such as in asset value and liabilities—on their balance sheet and earnings statement.

Stage 8: Putting it all together.

Assuming you've grasped the concept of investment risk, you'll be able to decide how important to you and the plan are such factors as preservation of capital, capital growth, ease of reinvestment, consistency of return, liquidity of assets and high current income.

Each bears its own risks. Treasury bills, for example, could be considered risky even though the principal isn't at risk. The T-bill carries with it reinvestment risk; you bear the risk that when a T-bill matures in 91 days, you might not be able to reinvest the proceeds at as high of a rate as you did previously. There is also inflation risk. Historically, T-bills have provided a return of less than one-half of one percent in excess of inflation. This is an example of a real world trade-off in risk vs. return.

When you're ready, state your long-term rate of return objective, as a percentage above inflation (as measured by the Consumer Price Index), or in absolute terms. You can state your risk constraints, either in relation to the overall market or in such terms as the amount of added risk you're willing to take on to increase the expected return by one percentage point. You also can include your diversification goals, which are connected to asset allocation—the subject of the next step.

Summing Up

We've thrust a lot of reasonably boring and technical information at you, but don't forget the key lesson: Separate the investment policy statement from the portfolio management function and, by all means, ask yourself these questions:

1. Where do I want to go from here? What do I want to accomplish with this portfolio? Do I want to guarantee a set benefit at retirement, as a defined benefit pension plan does? Do I want my individual investments to enable me to retire in a comfortable lifestyle by a certain age? Do I want to fund programs without depleting the asset base?

2. What tests must the investment policy withstand? How do I write it so it shapes the investments and so a portfolio manager will know exactly what I want? Is my policy long term, meaning can my policy be followed under any market conditions?

3. If this is an employee benefit fund, have I taken into account the needs and financial health of the corporation and the participants? Have I gotten such necessary data from my actuary as the interest-rate assumption and the salary assumption?

4. What rate of return (either in absolute or relative terms) do I need to achieve my goals?

5. Do I understand the historical performance of the various asset classes?

6. Do I understand investment risk or volatility?

7. What kind of risk am I willing to take to achieve my rate-of-return objective? (If you find you are not willing to take the amount of risk necessary to achieve that objective, go back and reexamine both. One has to change.)

8. Ask yourself: What was my immediate reaction to the Oct. 19, 1987, stock market crash?

   - If it was to dump stocks and get out of the market altogether, you probably should adopt a low-risk investment strategy and very conservative investment goals if it is appropriate for your fund.

   - If it was to reduce, but not eliminate, your stock portfolio, that was a normal reaction, and you probably can handle a middle-of-the-road investment policy with moderate investment goals.

- If it was to increase stock exposure in the belief that the crash made stocks a good buy, you probably are psychologically able to accept an aggressive investment policy if it is appropriate for the plan.

Your goal should be to achieve your targeted rate of return objectives without incurring more risk than you have decided you are willing to take. To do that, you must rid yourself of the notion that you need to keep up with the Joneses. The only investor you need to keep up with is yourself.

STEP 3

STEP 3:

Allocating Assets

*"A study of economics usually reveals that the
best time to buy anything is last year."*
MARTY ALLEN

D on't run out and hire a passel of money managers yet. Now
that you've formulated your rate of return objectives and your
tolerance for risk, there's one more investment policy matter:
You've got to decide what to do with the money you want to invest; that is, you must allocate the assets among various investment
classes and, perhaps, among various investment styles within those
classes.

This chapter will outline how to allocate your investable assets
among stocks, bonds, Treasury bills (and other cash equivalents)
and other asset classes. There are two distinct asset allocation considerations—long term, or strategic, and short term, or tactical. We
will address long-term allocation first.

Investment management professionals say investors make some
of their most costly mistakes in the area of asset allocation:

**Mistake #1: Trustees spend too much time on hiring and
firing managers and not enough time on
allocating assets.**

Perhaps because of the complexity of the subject matter, many trustees—plagued with too much to do and not enough time—need to be convinced to tackle asset allocation. Consider this: Many investment professionals believe asset allocation accounts for at least 80% of your portfolio's investment performance. That, in turn, means selecting individual stocks and bonds accounts for 20% or less of your total investment return. Therefore, trustees should expend the most time and energy on asset allocation decisions and less on hiring or firing money managers, the people who make the security selection within the asset classes.

Yet consultants say trustees aren't using their limited time effectively, devoting only about 5% of their time to asset allocation and far too much time on areas they can't control, such as manager performance.

Mistake #2:   Investors abdicate control over the decision.

Maybe you don't want to hire several specialty managers because you don't think you have the expertise to decide how much of your assets to give to equity managers and how much to give to fixed-income managers.

That's OK. But even when an investor intends to hire only one money manager for a balanced portfolio of stocks, bonds and cash, asset allocation probably should be a team decision. A few firms that call themselves balanced managers actually will make wide swings that can be as extreme as 100% in stocks, 100% in bonds or 100% in cash. That's a far cry from giving the balanced manager the discretion to move from a 50-50 asset allocation mix to 60-40, depending on market conditions. If you don't want to be fully invested (that is, have 100% of your money) in one asset class, you are going to have to be actively involved in the asset allocation decision from the beginning.

Suppose you hire two balanced managers? At the very least, sit down with them and get their recommendations. You probably will find areas they agree on, and you can question each about the areas where they differ. You and the managers can come away from those sessions knowing you had a meeting of the minds on how the portfolio managers should invest your assets among different classes. That's not to say you should tell them what stocks to buy—that's what you're paying them to decide—but you can give them a range (say, 30% to 50% of assets they manage for you) you'd feel comfortable with being invested in the stock market.

You don't want your managers to make decisions that cancel out each other or that serve cross purposes. For example, you might give half of your assets to each of two managers, aiming for them to allocate a total of 60% of your assets to stocks. If you don't discuss asset allocation with each, Manager A might put 60% into stocks, but Manager B might invest only 40% in stocks. That way, you wind up with only a 50% stock allocation, when you wanted 60%.

When investors forfeit their responsibility to set asset allocation, the resulting allocation can be too loose and might not be appropriate given the needs of the fund. One money manager remembers a client who allowed his firm to invest solely in growth stocks, which, typically, pay low dividends (and, therefore, provide little current income) because growth companies pump most of the profits back into the company. Only later did the manager learn the plan sponsor was a mature company with a high percentage of plan participants at or near retirement age. At the manager's urging, the asset allocation mix was changed to produce more current income.

As you learned from the last chapter, trustees have the responsibility of setting an investment policy that is consistent with the goals of the plan; determining asset allocation is the last step of that policy. Even if the manager has read the plan's investment policy statement, he/she might sign off on it without fully understanding such considerations as the funded status or the liquidity needs of the plan. The resulting asset allocation, done in isolation from information on the liabilities, may be too conservative and has a higher percentage allocation to fixed income than is necessary. When that happens, the sponsor later might have to increase contributions to the plan.

Mistake #3:   Asset allocation decisions are arbitrary.

An example of arbitrary asset allocation decision-making was cited by several investment consultants. Occasionally, they said, a new treasurer or corporate financial officer will take over and decide to make major changes in the asset allocation in order to make his or her mark on the fund. Employee benefit funds are more visible than ever before within the corporate structure, and the person who oversees those assets wants some visibility too.

Mistake #4:   Asset allocation decisions are extreme.

Some consultants tell of trustees putting 100% of assets in equities in the belief the fund will be around forever to make up any shortfall from unrewarded risk. But with takeovers, mergers, ac-quisitions and pension plan terminations, there's a good chance the fund won't be permanent. Another extreme is all bonds, which some investors consider to be less risky than other assets but which can underperform competitive asset classes for an extended period of time.

Even if you decide on a heavy allocation to one asset class, you can control some of the risk by mixing in Treasury bills or other assets with shorter maturities. One union fund, for example, had all of its assets in certificates of deposit. Trustees found their fund's asset growth was trailing that of its unfunded liability. The ultra conservative approach was digging an ever deeper hole. Over a year's time, the fund's consultants worked with trustees to move 60% of the assets into stocks, bonds and real estate, with 40% remaining in short-term investments to control risk.

Mistake #5:   Asset allocation decisions are made at the
wrong time.

John A. Vann, senior vice president for Dean Witter Reynolds' per-formance evaluation services, remembers when he tried to keep clients from making asset allocation decisions at the wrong time. He calls it his "most difficult sale ever made." In 1981-82, when money market funds were paying 20% interest, Vann fought to convince clients to buy guaranteed investment contracts (which are issued by insurance companies and pay a specified rate of return over a specified period) that would lock in interest rates of 17.3% for five to 10 years. "I couldn't convince them the 20% on money markets was short term," he laments. Experiences like that tell Vann investors make tactical decisions without a strategic, or long-range asset allocation plan.

Asset allocation decisions should be deliberate, thoughtful and proactive. They should not be reactive. One common, but potentially deadly, reaction is fueled by greed. Investors who should have known better sheepishly tell of watching the stock market climb for five years and, wanting a bigger piece of the action, changed tactics. In the late summer of 1987, they moved most of their short-term holdings into stock index funds, only to lose 20% to 25% when the market crashed a few short months later.

When it comes to making allocation decisions, many investors want to wait until everyone else has tested the waters. Says Mary Ann Johnson, president of Tremont Partners, a consulting firm: "Usually if you're last in, you miss the opportunity."

Mistake #6:   Assets are allocated by looking in the rearview mirror instead of out the windshield.

Gary P. Brinson, of Brinson Partners, understands why investors take this approach. "Everything is murky out of the windshield, but crystal clear in the rearview mirror." Still, he believes it is folly to spend too much time looking backward at what worked and what didn't work.

Instead, he says, investors should choose the forward path, hacking through the brush and undergrowth that obscures their vision. They can do so by accepting that all markets have well-defined characteristics and that normal asset allocation should be based on those normal characteristics, he asserts. Investors must learn about these characteristics—rates of return, volatility, diversification, inflation hedging—and, using those and their investment policies, should be able to make sound asset allocation decisions.

Traditionally, if recent past performance of the stock market has been poor, there's a low equity exposure in a typical asset allocation policy. In the mid-1970s, for example, many plan sponsors made very conservative asset allocation decisions following enactment of the Employee Retirement Income Security Act (ERISA) in 1974, which followed on the heels of a bear market. Immediately afterwards, a 10-year bull market began, and many funds were underexposed to stocks. The most recent example was in the aftermath of the October 1987 stock market meltdown, when some large funds sold all of their stocks. Since then, the market has risen substantially.

Asset allocation decisions are long term, not short term, and are based on the same conditions that guide general investment policy: funding requirements; the degree of volatility that's acceptable; long-term rates of return; and long-term asset-liability projections.

Mistake #7:   Believing you're too small to diversify.

Diversification, or spreading your assets across a range of investments, is considered by many investment professionals to be a mandate for investors. Diversification among asset classes is possible no matter how small your asset base. Even a smaller investor can obtain diversification by hiring a balanced manager who invests in more than one asset class.

Investors also can achieve diversification by using commingled funds, in which banks and insurance companies pool the assets of many investors, or by using mutual funds. Commingled and mutual funds offer investors a wide array of specialty investments, ranging from stock funds that specialize in one sector, such as utilities, to those that specialize in international bonds or real estate. As a rule, fees are lower for such funds than for specialty managers who might manage only separate accounts.

Too many middle-market investors take the easy way out of the diversification issue by believing they don't have enough money to invest in anything beyond stocks or bonds. Don't use the size of your asset base as an excuse.

Mistake #8:   Being too conservative.

"The biggest mistake they make is being too conservative, mainly in asset allocation," asserts consultant Bill Wurts, president of Wurts, Johnson & Co. He maintains the average equity exposure today is 46%, largely because many balanced managers got burned in the 1973-74 stock market and, after retreating, never returned to heavier stock exposure. "But I think a 60% allocation to stocks would be better." Many experts wouldn't agree with that level of stock commitment; in Step 2, we saw that researchers at Salomon Brothers leaned toward 30% in stocks to ensure a balance between reaching target goals and avoiding a loss. The level depends on the fund's needs, but the point is to ask yourself if you are being too conservative.

How To Allocate Assets The Right Way

Asset allocation plays a key role in achieving the risk profile you have decided is appropriate for your fund. The higher the risk level you and your fund can accept, the greater the amount of assets you can invest in stocks, for example. Asset allocation also determines the kind of managers you will select, rather than manager selection determining the asset allocation.

The first decision is: What asset classes will you include in the portfolio? Either on your own or with the help of a consultant, you probably are awash in risk and return data by now. But if you want one more opinion, here's how Roger G. Ibbotson and Gary P. Brinson, authors of *Investment Markets,* assess the various asset classes:[1]

---

1   Roger G. Ibbotson and Gary P. Brinson, *Investment Markets* (New York: McGraw-Hill Inc., 1987).

- Money invested in stocks would have doubled roughly every nine years since 1789.

- Bonds have beaten inflation, but with substantially lower returns than stocks.

- Cash returns closely match inflation.

- Over the long term, capital gains on real estate have about equaled the inflation rate, after allowing for depreciation.

- Foreign equity market returns have surpassed those of the United States during the past 25 years, with Asian equities returning an annualized 16% per year, vs. 10% for stocks on the New York Stock Exchange.

Of course, as we've stated before, the past is not necessarily a good predictor of the future, meaning there's no guarantee, for example, that foreign stocks will continue to outperform U.S. stocks.

Once you've chosen your asset classes, what weighting will each have within your portfolio?

Your pool of assets is a pie. Your job is to carve out a piece for stocks, a piece for bonds, etc. You can express those weightings in ranges, rather than in absolute terms. For example, instead of simply stating you want half your assets in stocks, you can state a range of, say, 40% to 60%. Ranges give you and your managers the latitude to take advantage of investment opportunities that will come up after your policy and asset allocation are in place. If you, your consultant or your money manager has some specific insight about the short-term performance of a particular investment class, that range will allow you to take advantage of the opportunity.

The percentage allocations are targets. You could already have money invested in such a way that your portfolio will be out of balance with your stated asset allocation. That's OK. You can achieve those targets over time, either by selling overweighted holdings (not dumping them at fire-sale prices) or by allocating cash flow (such as contributions and investment income) to the underweighted asset classes.

If your current asset mix is a long way away from your target, you can set a timetable for reaching your goals. Perhaps you'll want 10% to 20% of your assets in real estate within five years, yet you have no assets currently in real estate. You can tell your managers you expect to invest 2% to 4% of your assets in real estate each year, with the money coming from a reduction in the allocation to a currently overweighted asset class or from cash flow.

Once you've decided on the asset classes and how much to invest in each, there's one more major decision: Which investment strategies and kinds of money managers should you employ?

Those decisions are part of the asset allocation process, and precede manager selection. Kenneth L. Fisher, president of Fisher Investments, Inc., says one of the most common mistakes investors make is to use the manager search phase to determine manager styles. "When you look at the managers (an investor) has in the semifinals, and there are different styles, you know they're using the search to figure out what style they want. They should have done that earlier in the process," Fisher notes.

The basic types of managers, discussed in detail in Step 4 and Step 9, include:

- Active stock, or equity, managers
- Active bond, or fixed-income, managers
- Balanced (stock and bond) managers
- Passive equity or index-fund managers
- Passive bond or indexed and/or dedicated managers
- Real estate managers
- International equity managers
- International fixed-income managers
- Venture capital managers

Here's a sample of the kind of choices among managers you might have to make: A fund that has allocated assets only to stocks and bonds might want to hire managers to run balanced accounts, which invest in both. As an example, William F. Quinn, president of AMR Investment Services, talks about his experience with a mature plan with $45 million in assets. That plan hired four balanced managers, telling them to generally keep about 60% in stocks and 40% in bonds. But the actual asset mix can vary because of changing market conditions: In late September 1988, for example, the mix was 45% stocks, 45% bonds and 10% cash.

For a start-up firm with a young work force and small liability, Quinn recommends hiring several balanced managers with the same split for a total of 80% of the assets, and adding an equity manager for 20% of the assets. That way, the equity exposure is increased, but the fund still gets the benefits of balanced management.

Others don't believe in balanced managers, contending it makes more sense to hire equity specialists to manage stocks and fixed-income specialists to manage bonds. Since balanced managers tend to have more expertise in one asset class than in another, they say, why not hire the best equity manager and the best fixed-income manager. That doesn't eliminate a balanced manager from the competition, by the way. Most balanced managers also handle pure equity and/or pure fixed-income accounts.

As another example, trustees concerned about preservation of capital might decide to hire an equity manager who specializes in value stocks and a bond manager who specializes in defensive bond portfolio management.

Still another option would be to put the bulk of the equity assets in a stock index fund, the bulk of the fixed-income assets in a bond index fund, and place smaller amounts with a specialty equity manager (perhaps one who invests in growth stocks) and a specialty bond manager (perhaps one who invests in high-yield, or junk bonds). But some consultants and investment management professionals advise middle-market investors against indexing because of the potentially large losses in a bear market. This is because an index fund is always fully invested, whereas active managers often will attempt to reduce their stock holdings and invest in short-term bonds or money market instruments when they are uncertain about the stock market. As a result, portfolios managed by active managers often decline less than the market when the market drops. Conversely, studies show many managers don't outperform the indexes in up markets, in part because they always have at least a minimal cash position no matter how fully invested they are, and cash pulls down returns in a bull market.

Quinn argues against hiring only one investment manager, no matter how small the asset. "I think it's worth paying up," meaning paying higher fees for several managers rather than having all of your money managed by one. "I've never seen a manager who's always right. If I have $10 million, I'd have four $2.5 million accounts. I know I'm paying a percent higher than I should, but I'm avoiding catastrophe."

He cites a manager he had hired for the American Airlines pension fund (whose investments Quinn oversees) who had been right for six years in a row. "We thought he was infallible," Quinn said. As the stock market rose in 1982, he remembers, the manager thought the rise would be short-lived, so he got out of the market, first buying defensive stocks and later switching to bonds and cash. "If he had been the only guy managing money for us, he would've killed us."

Say you've made the decision to put 50% of your assets in equities. Now, you have to decide how to parcel out the money to the various investment styles for stocks. Asghar Alam, head of Wyatt Asset Services in Europe, suggests fashioning an asset allocation plan that would be specific enough to say, "Of the 50% in equities, half will be in value stocks and half will be in growth stocks. Within the assets allocated to growth stocks, I want to concentrate on health care and high-technology companies. Within the assets allocated to value stocks, I want to concentrate on basic industry stocks." Too often, a client just says, "We want 50% in equities, and we want the money to be well-diversified." And, naturally, the client doesn't define well-diversified.

"The biggest hurdle in switching to multiple managers is that the plan sponsor has to take on the asset allocation decision," Alam believes. If trustees "have a balanced manager, they can let him do the asset allocation. If they want an equity and a fixed-income manager, they'll have to do the work," he says. Trustees also will have to accept responsibility for their decisions.

Some asset allocation decisions include minimums and maximums on the number of securities a manager may purchase. An equity manager, for example, might be instructed to purchase a minimum of 30 companies, with no more than 5% in any one company. Investors often put in ceilings, but forget the floors. If you have too many stocks in your portfolio—more than 50—you might have an index fund though you are paying for active management. If you have too few—fewer than 20—you might be taking more risk than you want to take.

The more asset classes and investment styles you add, the more possibilities you have. A decision to commit to real estate also involves decisions about whether to invest in commercial/office, retail, multifamily, land or hotel and developmental or existing properties. Every asset class has a host of its equivalent balanced managers and a bunch of specialty ones as well. Plus, of course, there are commingled funds—in which your assets are pooled with money from other investors—and mutual funds in addition to separate accounts, in which your money is handled separate from other investors'.

Strategic Versus Tactical Asset Allocation

Your asset allocation decisions, like your investment objectives, will not be static. You'll be reviewing them to see how they work for you. The long-term allocation decisions are sometimes called strategic asset allocation; the short-term ones, tactical asset allocation or active asset allocation, two terms that have caught on with investors since the October 1987 stock market crash.

You'll have to decide if you want to expend the time and energy to actively manage the asset allocation process. The idea is that markets don't always behave normally, so you might want to have at least one investment manager who can make a change in the asset mix that reflects current conditions. This manager sometimes is referred to as a "swing" manager. The idea works this way: If you can tolerate an equity exposure of up to, say, 70%, give 50% of your total assets to an equity manager that is adept at security selection, and 20% of your total assets to an asset allocation manager. That way you have a band of about 20%, and will hit the 70% equity exposure only when the asset allocator perceives the stock market is the optimum place to be.

Noel Feldman, partner in Hewitt Associates, says short-term asset shifts are the purview of the money manager: "The plan sponsor doesn't know how, and if consultants were that good at it we'd be in the money management business."

A growing number of investment managers specialize in active asset allocation. Some move across only two markets, most commonly stocks and cash. Others move among stocks, bonds and cash; still others use many markets, including real estate and international.

Brinson Partners specializes in active asset allocation, which president and chief investment officer Gary P. Brinson characterizes as "deviating temporarily from the normal policy mix. It is based upon judgments that one or more asset classes are in a state of disequilibrium with respect to the investment characteristics that were utilized in forming the policy mix." (Brinson and others bemoan the confusion between active or tactical asset allocation and market timing because some money managers previously thought of as market timers now call themselves tactical asset allocators. He contends market timers alter an asset mix due to some forecast of future price changes, and make those changes in an attempt to take advantage of what the market will pay for a certain security over the short term.)

In a paper on asset allocation that was circulated within the investment community, Brinson gave these examples of markets in which a normal asset mix could have been altered because of deviations or disequilibrium: In the early 1980s, interest rates on long-term government bonds exceeded 14%, which was a non-normal risk/return relationship, so bond positions should have been increased to lock up those high returns, and stock positions should have been reduced, even though the decision to buy those bonds was not dependent on a subsequent decline in interest rates; in early 1985, international fixed-income markets and their currency components were undervalued; in 1983, domestic small-capitalization stocks were overvalued; in 1985, some sectors of the real estate market were overvalued; in the summer of 1987, the domestic stock market was extremely overvalued; and in late 1988, the Japanese stock market was extremely overvalued.

In those cases, active asset allocation decisions focused on "understanding current conditions in the various asset classes and judging whether current investment characteristics were in or out of the equilibrium state that was utilized in determining the investor's normal asset allocation mix," he said.

Case Studies On Allocating Assets

When it comes to asset allocation, there's no formula, no magic. Just hard work. Each fund must fashion its own asset allocation to meet its goals and objectives, although a consultant, who has been down this road many times before, surely will have some suggestions once he/she becomes familiar with your fund and your objectives. Brinson Partners has an optimal portfolio allocation which we've shown on page 57. Use this only as a guide, however.

Even after much cajoling, most consultants wouldn't reveal any "typical" asset allocation for an employee benefit fund. Gerald F. Bott, of Merrill Lynch, gave at least a rough idea. Using historical rates of return data, he suggested an investor wanting to achieve an 8% rate of return (before inflation) should put 20% of assets in equities and 80% in fixed income. An investor seeking a 10% return, he said, could increase the equity exposure to 30% and decrease the fixed-income exposure to 70%.

Other consultants think the leap is more dramatic, although they would speak only in generalities. The lower the rate of return objective, the higher the number of choices. As the return objective increases, your choices become more limited, with more and more money allocated to stocks.

Consultants to foundations and endowments, however, generally push for higher equity allocations than are common among employee benefit funds. That's because they need returns high enough to compensate for any erosion of principal that results from spending programs. "You have to have an 80-20 mix (between stocks and bonds) if you spend a lot of the capital," explains Ned A. Joachimi, chairman of Wellesley Group, Inc. "The equity arena is where the action is" on returns. Other consultants say their equity range for foundations and endowments is 50%-75%, again depending on their spending needs.

MULTIPLE MARKETS INDEX

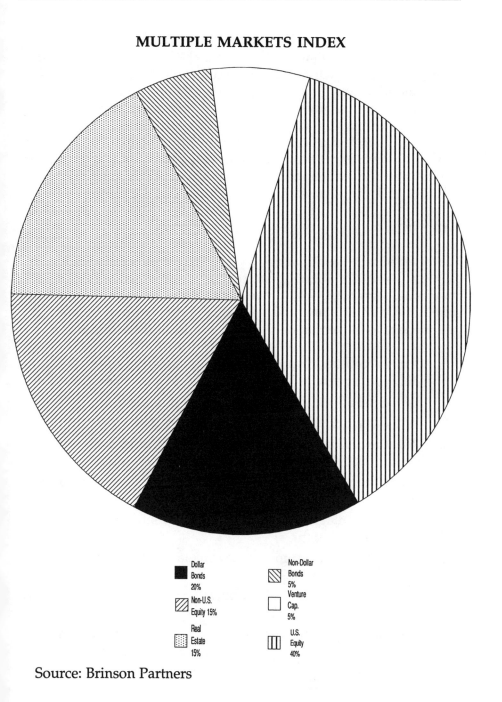

Source: Brinson Partners

Leonard Armstrong, vice president and consultant for Merrill Lynch, had one foundation that had 100% of its money in short-term instruments such as certificates of deposit and Treasury bills. The foundation was giving away 8% to 10% of its money each year, but was earning no more than 5% to 6% (before inflation). To bring the income and payout closer together, Armstrong worked with the trustees to change the asset allocation to 3% in venture capital; 20% to 30% in passive equities through a stock index fund; 10% in fixed income; and the remainder in active equity management.

Summing Up

The asset allocation decision—whether to invest in stocks, bonds, cash equivalents, real estate, international and other asset classes— is the single-most important investment decision you will make, accounting for an estimated 80% of your portfolio's performance. As you prepare to make that decision, ask yourself these questions:

1. Am I accepting responsibility for making the asset allocation decision, even when I have balanced money managers?
2. Will asset allocation be done before I hire managers?
3. Will these decisions be proactive, rather than reactive?
4. Are my decisions based on the return objectives and risk tolerances I have outlined in my investment policy?
5. What asset classes will I include? Do I have historical rates of return data on which to evaluate each class?
6. What percentage of my assets will I put into each investment class I have chosen?
7. How will I instruct my money managers to reach the target allocations I have set?
8. Do I understand the risk implications of the asset mix I have chosen?
9. Do I understand the difference between strategic and tactical asset allocation? Am I willing to invest the time to actively manage the asset allocation process?

STEP 4

STEP 4:

Understanding Manager Styles

*"If you walk like a duck...quack like a duck...
you're a duck."*
POPULARIZED BY THE BUSH ADMINISTRATION

For years, trying to purchase beef at a meat counter was akin to unraveling a mystery. What one store called a New York roast, another called a Seven Bone roast, yet both were nothing more than chuck roasts. Today, a chuck roast is called a chuck roast somewhere on the label, thanks to the U.S. Department of Agriculture's push to standardize labeling.

In money management, however, no one is standardizing the labeling of investment managers. That task falls to you, the consumer. This chapter will explain what the different investment management styles are and how they differ. But before you learn to differentiate among styles, be aware of the most common mistake investors make in the area of manager styles:

Mistake #1: Investors don't understand what the manager does and how he/she does it.

When Phil Schneider was a pension executive with United Air Lines, the pilots' fund hired Batterymarch Financial Management as a value manager. Schneider, now head of the U.S. practice for Wyatt Asset Services, Inc., recalls, at the time, "the value was in small stocks, so Batterymarch bought small stocks." When the value wasn't there anymore, Dean LeBaron, the legendary head of Batterymarch, shifted to other stocks. Returns declined, probably because LeBaron couldn't find value in stocks that were as high-flying as small stocks had been. Trustees complained, Schneider said. "They thought Batterymarch was hired as a small stock manager, and LeBaron wasn't buying small stocks anymore." Naturally, Schneider had to remind his trustees of the reason they hired Batterymarch.

In the late 1970s and very early 1980s, dozens of institutional investors hired Houston's Fayez Sarofim because of his expertise in energy stocks. At the time they hired him, Sarofim's performance was soaring because oil company stocks were booming. Then the price of oil took a dive, and Sarofim's star shined less brightly. Some clients were so upset they fired him. But many of the more sophisticated clients reacted more rationally: They remembered they hired him to specialize in a specific sector of the market, and he was doing what he said he would do.

These are but two of an endless collection of examples that underscore the importance of understanding managers' styles.

You also need to learn about the methodologies and investment processes within each style. For example, to understand a low p/e-style manager, you need to understand, first, that such a manager identifies and purchases stocks that have a lower price/earnings ratio than the price/earnings ratio of the market. Then, you need to understand how that manager systematically ferrets out such low p/e stocks, often using a computer screening process. All this should be thoroughly explained to you before you hire a manager.

What's important is that you understand what a manager is trying to do and how he/she goes about doing it.

There's one other common mistake:

Mistake #2:   Investors assume one style will always be in favor.

Every manager style has its rotation or cycle. Some say a typical capital market cycle is 45 months from trough to trough, and that no manager style will perform well for more than two-thirds of that cycle, or 2 1/2 years. Others say a manager performs well for six to eight quarters (1 1/2 to 2 years) and poorly for eight quarters (or two years). Whatever the amount of time, the key is to understand that manager performance goes in cycles.

Different styles take different amounts of time to prove successful. Some value managers, who buy out-of-favor stocks, say they need five years to produce good, annualized returns.

Often, the degree of the manager's success depends on when in the market cycle you hire the firm: If interest rates begin to fall a few months after you hire a manager who specializes in long-term bonds, your portfolio's returns will be high simply because you were lucky enough to have hired the firm at the right time. Had you hired that same firm and interest rates rose, your returns wouldn't be so great. At the beginning of 1989, for example, there was an inverted yield curve, meaning short-term interest rates were as high or higher than long-term interest rates. A manager specializing in short-term instruments such as Treasury bills would have turned in a far better performance than when the yield curve behaved normally.

Indeed, it's because no one investment style always produces topflight returns that investors blend investment styles by hiring two or more money managers, each with a different style. The goal is to have the second manager complement, not duplicate, the first manager's style and, therefore, the first manager's likely performance.

Active Versus Passive

Probably the first decision when choosing manager styles is whether you want your portfolio actively managed, passively managed, or whether you want some combination of the two. In active management, portfolio managers try to beat the returns offered by the market as a whole by making timely buy and sell decisions based on their investment approaches and strategies and on their economic and market outlooks. In passive management, securities are traded less frequently and, therefore, fewer decisions are made once the portfolio has been established.

Some investors, particularly jumbo pension funds with billions of dollars in assets, have chosen passive management for the bulk of their money, believing their sheer size would prevent them from outperforming the market. (They subscribe to the theory: "We can't beat the market; we *are* the market.") That is called a core portfolio. Then, they set aside a smaller percentage of assets to place with specialty managers in the hope their active management styles will add value, or cause overall investment performance to be better than the market.

Although most of this chapter will deal with active management styles, it's important to have at least a basic understanding of passive management.

The most common form of passive management is indexing, in which assets are invested the same way an index, or basket of securities, is invested. In its simplest form, an index fund mirrors a popular index, such as the Standard & Poor's 500, Russell 2000 or Wilshire 5000 stock indexes, meaning your indexed assets would be invested, proportionately, in the same stocks contained in the index. In a pure S&P 500 stock index fund, for example, if transportation stocks make up 15% of the S&P 500, then 15% of your indexed assets would be in transportation stocks. More specifically, if ABC Airlines makes up 1% of the S&P 500, then 1% of your assets would be invested in ABC Airlines. Such an approach is not without a price, however. Even though stocks in an S&P 500 index wouldn't be actively traded, the fund would incur transaction costs in the course of buying and selling securities to invest cash flow and as stocks drop out of, or are added to, the S&P 500. Because of those costs, some managers tailor (or customize) index funds to mirror a particular index without holding all of the stocks in the index.

On the fixed-income side, there are bond index funds that replicate popular bond indexes the same way stock index funds replicate stock indexes. In addition, there are two other forms of passive management—immunization and dedication—both of which are used to produce a predictable flow of income in order to meet a defined stream of benefit payments.

An immunized bond portfolio blends bond maturities in such a way that a change in interest rates affects the value of the portfolio the same way it affects the amount of liabilities the portfolio is designed to meet. For example, if there is a rise in interest rates that reduces the value of the portfolio by 10%, that interest rate hike also reduces the amount of the liabilities by 10%, so assets and liabilities remain matched. A dedicated bond portfolio is one that matches cash flows (investment income and return of principal as bonds mature) from the portfolio with payments to retirees. Such a portfolio is dedicated to the group of participants known as retired lives.

Read on for specifics that will help you with some of the basics of stock and bond investment management styles. The information that follows can get pretty technical. Trustees don't need to spend much of their valuable time memorizing this information, which isn't as crucial as understanding asset allocation. But for those who are involved in choosing multiple managers, a basic understanding of investment approaches and manager styles is important.

Stock Approaches

There are two basic approaches or processes to selecting stocks: top-down and bottom-up. Top-down begins with economic forecasts for some future period, such as a year, then determines which market sectors or industries likely would prosper within that economic framework. Individual companies are purchased within those favored industries or market sectors.

A bottom-up approach looks at the market on a stock-by-stock basis and buys those stocks with the most attractive risk/reward relationships. Little attention is given to overall economic trends. Typically, a bottom-up manager examines the fundamentals of a large number of stocks, trying to identify ones that meet his or her specific criteria. Often these criteria are programmed into computers along with financial data about a great number of stocks in the manager's universe. Some managers include the entire New York Stock Exchange in their universe. The computers then screen for the stocks that best meet the criteria, whittling the list to, say, the 200 best stocks, from which a portfolio of 35 or 40 might be selected after further research.

Stock Analysis

Some managers emphasize fundamental analysis; others emphasize technical analysis. Fundamental analysis involves an examination of company and industry data (nonmarket data) in order to determine the intrinsic value of a company. A manager then buys those stocks whose prices are below the fundamental or intrinsic value of the company.

Pure technical analysis ignores such "fundamentals" as earnings and revenue growth, instead relying on supply and demand factors, with the manager buying stocks that are in the most demand or with the most favorable price action. The technical analyst looks at market and stock price trends, trying to discover predictive patterns.

Equity Styles

Despite the proliferation of labels, many investment professionals say there basically are only two kinds of fundamentally based active equity management. One emphasizes value, one emphasizes growth.

Value managers buy stocks whose current market price is substantially less than the calculated real value. There are a number of different ways to calculate the real value of a company. Some money managers look at the value of a company's assets; some look at its cash flow; some put a value on its earnings per share during the past five or 10 years; some project earnings per share for five years into the future and discount the earnings stream back to a present value; some use a combination of these approaches. Of course, everyone defines "value" in a different way, and it would be difficult to find a money manager who believes in buying "non-value" stocks.

Except for the discounted projected earnings method, most value approaches are based on the work of Benjamin Graham and David Dodd. This is what managers mean when they speak of a "Graham and Dodd" approach to investing. Graham and Dodd made security analysis a systematic skill. They provided a series of rules and ratios to apply when valuing companies. Interestingly, many of their rules are used by appraisers today to value privately held companies for sale.

Growth managers buy shares in companies whose growth rates in sales and earnings have been, or are expected to be, greater than most other companies. These companies typically are reinvesting profits in the business, so they aren't paying big dividends today, but the bet is these actions will result in future increases in the stock price.

Some managers say they are low p/e (price/earnings) managers, meaning they buy stocks whose price/earnings ratios are lower than others because, historically, stocks with low p/es have had, over long periods of time, returns that are superior to those of stocks with high p/es. Low p/e managers look for companies whose p/e is low because they are overlooked or out of favor.

Still other managers say they are emerging growth stock managers, meaning they buy stock in companies that are less mature than seasoned growth companies. Others say they are income managers, meaning they look for stocks with above-average dividend yield (obtained by dividing the yearly dividend by the price), or they emphasize stability and growth of dividends.

Consultant Ned A. Joachimi, chairman of Wellesley Group, divides managers into five categories: value-income; growth and income; quality growth; lower-capitalization; and aggressive or emerging growth.

Consultant Bill Wurts, president of Wurts, Johnson & Co., agrees there are two types of equity managers, but he categorizes their styles differently: those who take above-average risk and those who take below-average risk. In his opinion, the styles that take below-average risk are low p/e, income, timing and contrarian. Styles that take above-average risk are growth, smaller capitalization and emerging growth and sector rotational.

Noel Feldman, partner in Hewitt Associates, puts managers into two others camps: asset allocation and security selection. "Is their first decision to be fully invested at all times, or is their first decision how much to allocate" is the question Feldman uses to separate managers into the two sides.

Everyone has heard of market timers. Market timers themselves disagree over how to define their style. One description involves the willingness to move a large percentage of assets either into the stock market and out of cash or into cash and out of stocks. That means a market timer can go from being 100% invested in the stock market to being 100% invested in cash during a reasonably short period of time. The idea is to move as much as possible out of the asset class or category that currently is producing the worst returns and into the asset class or category producing the best returns.

Mercer Meidinger Hansen, Inc. is among the consulting firms with many different style categories. A committee of the firm's consultants from around the country honed and reshaped what the firm calls its "manager strategy codes." The codes were used to develop peer groups of managers to help assess relative performance within a particular style.

"There's a tendency to have too few or too many categories of style," notes Mercer Meidinger Hansen's Terry Dennison, who coordinated the manager strategy code process. If an investor uses too many categories, Dennison says, the peer groups within each category are too small to make meaningful comparisons. If too few categories are used, he adds, an investor who wants to compare oranges to oranges ends up comparing all citrus fruits.

Here, reprinted with permission, are Mercer Meidinger Hansen's new manager strategy codes:

Equity value managers seek investments whose potential is temporarily unrecognized by other investors. Such managers invest in companies whose assets, future cash flows, products or services are overly discounted relative to the broader market. The key to an equity value manager's success is to properly identify those issues that are, in fact, currently undervalued by others. The portfolio of an equity value manager will exhibit a consistent bias to these types of issues. Economic sector and industry allocations can be either concentrated or widely diversified. Their p/e ratios will be less than the S&P 500, and their yields will be greater than the S&P 500.

Equity growth managers seek investments whose future potential for growth is above the growth expectation for stocks in general. Companies with new technologies, well-positioned in rapidly growing industries or with a proprietary product or service that will provide above-average earnings growth are the types of holdings found in a growth portfolio. The portfolio can be either concentrated or widely diversified. The key to a growth manager's success is to properly identify those issues that do, in fact, achieve higher earnings growth rates. Growth portfolios generally will have projected earnings, p/e ratios and plow-back ratios (the amount of profit the company puts back into the company, instead of paying it out to shareholders) greater than the S&P 500.

Equity small-capitalization managers seek investments in smaller capitalization issues to capture the inherently greater growth potential of smaller companies. Portfolios with more than 50% of their value invested in the issues of small-capitalization companies would fall into this category. The manager might use a variety of investment strategies to attempt to add value. The key to the small-capitalization manager's success is to invest in companies whose business strategy results in the dramatic growth of the company, which is recognized in the stock price. Issues with capitalizations in the bottom quartile (or bottom 25%) of the major market's comprehensive index are considered small capitalization issues.

Equity sector rotational managers seek to position the portfolio in the sectors of the market that will be most favorably affected by future economic events. The strategy is executed using a top-down approach. The portfolio can have either value or growth characteristics, but will be concentrated in one or more economic sectors. These concentrations will change through time as the manager's analysis indicates different economic sectors will benefit from future events. Properly predicting economic events and their impact on stock prices is the key to a sector rotator's success. A sector rotator's portfolio will consistently overweight or underweight at least two or three economic sectors by as much as 50%. These weightings will change over time, sometimes quite dramatically.

Equity market timing managers seek to position the portfolio in or out of the market based on expectations regarding the future direction of the market. These expectations are based on an analysis of fundamental data, technical data or both. Moving the portfolio substantially out of down markets and into up markets is the key to the market timer's success. Moves in and out of the market can be executed either in the cash, options or futures market. Stock selection is secondary, and can be done using a variety of strategies including indexing. Portfolio moves that result in more than 50% of the portfolio being pulled out of stocks in anticipation of a market downturn qualify the manager as a market timer.

Equity broadly diversified or core managers don't make significant bets away from the S&P 500 index in terms of economic sector or industry exposure. They try to beat the market by buying lots of stocks that do slightly better than the market—hitting lots of singles, not going for home runs. While some overweighting and underweighting of economic sectors and industries can occur in the portfolio, these will result from the manager's stock selection process and will not represent a deliberate attempt to bias the portfolio toward growth, low p/e or some economic theme. These managers have economic sector allocations that are between 0.5 and two times that of the market; the stocks they buy have betas that range between 0.95 and 1.05 (whereas the market has a beta of 1.0); the stocks in their portfolios have p/e ratios between 90% and 110% of the S&P 500; and the stocks have market capitalizations that are not less than 75% of the market's.

Equity index managers seek to equal the return of an index, such as the S&P 500. The beta would be the same as the index the manager seeks to replicate.

Equity specialized or narrowly focused managers seek to add value by focusing on a narrow area, or market segment, and developing the expertise to know that niche better than other investors. A manager who invests only in utility stocks or in convertibles (bonds or preferred stock that are convertible into shares of common stocks at a fixed price and at the option of the bondholder, and are often viewed as equity investments) are two examples. Superior knowledge of the area of focus is the manager's key to success.

Equity eclectic managers are those that cannot be reasonably put into any of the other categories.

There are many, many variations on equity styles. Don't accept at face value whatever style a firm tells you it follows: Find out what it means and the process used to follow that style.

Bond Management Styles

Some investment professionals contend there are actually only two styles of managing fixed-income assets: Either buy long-term instruments or short ones. Others divide bond managers into two other styles: those that move up and down the yield curve (the curve showing the interest rates being paid on bonds of different maturities at any given time) and those that swap securities.

Fixed-income managers that move up and down the yield curve are trying to forecast interest rates with the belief that most of the returns from bonds come from what interest rates do. That is, managers try to increase the portfolio's holdings of long-term bonds when they expect interest rates to decline and increase the holdings of short-term bonds when interest rates are expected to rise. They follow this approach because when interest rates decline, long-term bonds with high interest rates increase in value, and the portfolio can lock in capital gains. On the other hand, holding short-term bonds when rates rise protects the portfolio from declines in price that long-term bonds suffer. In addition, it permits the manager to keep reinvesting in higher and higher interest rates as the short-term notes mature every 30 or 60 days.

An interest-rate-anticipation strategy can be enormously profitable when successful. In early 1982, when long-term interest rates were 15%, the head of a jumbo public pension fund guessed interest rates had peaked, and moved the fund heavily into long-term bonds. A year later, long-term interest rates had dropped substantially, and the fund had a gain of $2 billion. Such timing, however, is difficult to achieve consistently.

The second kind of fixed-income manager concedes there's no way to be consistently accurate at predicting the direction of interest rates. This manager chooses to pursue the premium that comes from swapping among securities, like a sector rotator does, without being concerned with the yield curve. This is possible because the bond market is so large and complex that the market prices of two similar bonds can be quite different. A manager can sell the higher-priced one and buy the lower-priced one and still be earning the same interest.

Using computers, bond swappers look for two very similar bonds that either have the same interest rate but sell at different prices, or that have different interest rates but sell at the same price. For example, suppose Utility A issued a bond that matures in June 2005, with a 9% coupon. Because interest rates have risen since the bond was issued, the Utility A bond now sells for 96 (96% of face value, with face value typically being $1,000). Suppose Utility B, which carries the same credit rating as Utility A, also issued a bond with a 9% coupon and matures in July 2005. The Utility B bond sells for 94. The market has inefficiently priced the two virtually identical issues, perhaps because of the one month difference in maturity, or perhaps because Utility A is better known than Utility B. A bond-swapping manager would sell the bond of Utility A and buy the bond of Utility B, getting a higher effective yield because the interest rate is the same, yet the amount of dollars actually invested is smaller.

Another type of bond manager generally buys bonds of the same general maturity (long, intermediate or short), but rotates the sectors (government vs. corporate or industrial vs. utility vs. financial) from which the bonds are bought. There is a historical relationship between the interest rates paid by U.S. government bonds and corporate bonds of various ratings. When times are good, that relationship (called the spread) narrows. Investors do not demand such a large premium for holding corporates. When times are uncertain, the spread widens. In changing times, the sector rotating bond manager can profit by correctly predicting whether the spread will widen or narrow.

Still others buy a well-diversified portfolio of junk bonds, fixed-income securities that don't qualify as investment grade but, because of their lower ratings and higher risk, pay much higher yields than investment-grade ones. Some junk bond managers buy bonds issued by fast-growing companies too new to have their credit worthiness rated (by one of the bond rating agencies, such as Standard & Poor's or Moody's); others buy bonds in companies with financial difficulties, where the manager sees the opportunity of a turnaround or at least enough of an improvement to justify the risk.

Some investment professionals say there are four fixed-income approaches: focusing on interest rate changes; identifying the most attractive sectors to invest in; focusing on trading anomalies to gain something in quality or maturity that boosts return; and a combination of some or all of the other three styles.

Here's how Mercer Meidinger Hansen describes its fixed-income manager strategies:

Fixed-income/interest index managers invest to achieve the return of an index. Assets can be invested in any manner (by sector, quality, coupon or maturity) to replicate the index return. The duration (the weighted average maturity of the bond's stream of payments) of the portfolio generally will fall within a narrow range around that of the index, although returns can replicate that of the index without duration matching.

Fixed-income/interest low-quality managers invest 50% or more of assets in fixed-income securities rated below investment grade either by Standard & Poor's Corp. or Moody's Investors Service. These securities commonly are called high-yield or junk bonds.

Fixed-income/interest mechanical strategies managers invest in an immunized or dedicated manner (as explained earlier in this chapter) or in variations on these strategies. Asset deployment is based on directly covering underlying liabilities such as benefit payments or hospital fixed–costs. This classification can cover portfolios with exact cash matching to duration matching and with frequent to infrequent portfolio rebalancings.

Fixed-income/interest short-term managers buy bonds whose average maturity consistently falls in the one- to three-year range; they achieve returns by quality/coupon/sector swapping.

Fixed-income/interest intermediate managers invest in securities whose average maturity consistently falls in the three- to seven-year range. They too achieve returns by swapping among sectors, coupons or quality.

Fixed-income/interest long-term managers buy securities whose average maturity consistently falls in the greater than seven-year range; they achieve returns by the same kind of swapping done by short-term and intermediate managers.

Fixed-income interest rate anticipation managers achieve returns by significant adjustments to the average maturity of their holdings in anticipation of changes in the yield curve. Significant adjustments are defined to be from or to average maturities of less than three years to or from maturities greater than seven years.

Fixed-income/interest specialized managers invest in specialized markets, ranging from certain government agency securities (such as Ginnie Maes, issued by the Government National Mortgage Association), junk bond convertibles or guaranteed investment contracts in the secondary market.

Balanced Management Styles

Balanced managers typically balance and rebalance holdings between and among stocks, bonds and cash equivalents, depending on their evaluation of economic and market conditions and on the investors' own guidelines.

Many middle-market investors begin their adventure in money management by hiring a balanced manager to ensure exposure to the major capital markets. Then, as their assets grow, they might hire a second one. Perhaps they'll give each manager a different asset allocation range, with Manager A permitted to invest up to 50% in stocks and Manager B up to 70%.

According to Mercer Meidinger Hansen, there are fewer balanced manager strategy codes than there are codes for stock or bond managers. They are:

Balanced tactical/dynamic allocation managers hold a single portfolio balanced between two or more asset classes based on portfolio reviews at stated intervals and associated portfolio rebalancings. The investment manager has full discretion to make asset allocation shifts among allowable asset classes.

Balanced managers with other methods of allocation are the more traditional balanced managers. They manage a single portfolio balanced between two or more asset classes that doesn't involve tactical or dynamic allocation procedures. Instead, allocations are based on a manager's or client's longer-term outlook on financial or economic trends. Shifts in allocations will occur, but not at stated intervals. The investment manager has full discretion to move between asset classes, generally within allowable ranges.

Summing Up

Once trustees and others responsible for overseeing investment portfolios set investment policy and settle on allocations to the various asset classes, they must understand the various investment styles before they hire an investment manager. The most important lessons here are to understand what a manager does and how he or she does it, and that manager styles are cyclical, so no investment style always will be in favor.

Among the questions to ask yourself:

1. Do I understand the difference between passive and active management in equities and fixed income?
2. Do I understand the top-down and bottom-up stock approaches?
3. Do I understand fundamental and technical stock analysis?
4. Can I differentiate among the major styles of equity and fixed-income investing?

STEP 5

Selecting The Right Managers

"But many that are first shall be last;
and the last shall be first."
MATTHEW 19:30

There's no mystery to hiring a money manager. The complexities of the investment management process, combined with the industry's affinity for jargon (which we demystify in Step 10) appear to make the task more difficult than it is. Remember, the key word here is hiring.

As a businessman or businesswoman, you've undoubtedly made hundreds of hiring decisions. Treat this one the same. Hiring an investment manager is no different than hiring an engineer. Both deal with complex, sophisticated technical information. But that need not get in the way of the hiring process. You still need to get a resume, check credentials and references, conduct interviews and make a choice.

It's as simple as that.

Now, some questions for those who have been through the manager selection process before. Have you ever hired an investment manager because:

- The firm's past investment performance was too good to pass up?

- The manager seemed to have the Midas touch, and was clearly a "hot" firm?

- The client contact (your link to the firm) was particularly attentive and, perhaps, even persistent in pursuing you?

- You chose the firm that made the best presentation?

- Another investor, either a friend or someone whose opinion you respect, strongly recommended hiring the firm?

- In the case of banks and insurance companies, you or your company already had an existing relationship?

- The firm would be a manager for all seasons, investing all of your assets and relieving you of the burden of deciding how much money to allocate to different investments?

- The firm's fees were lower than other firms'?

If you answered "yes" to one or more questions, you could be jeopardizing your portfolio's performance by hiring investment managers for the wrong reasons. In the following pages, you'll learn the dos and don'ts of hiring a money manager, first by reading about the most common mistakes investors make in their search for the right manager and, second, by discovering the correct steps to take.

Mistake #1:   Past performance is too good to pass up.

Far too many investors believe they've done all their homework if they've received impressive performance numbers from the candidates. Indeed, performance is more of a reason to exclude managers than to include them. Once you've narrowed down the field to your finalists, it's reasonable to assume all of them have good performance, or they wouldn't have made it that far in your search. That should tell you now is the time to look behind and beyond the performance numbers.

Some investors feel they need confirmation that Manager A is a good manager, as if their own objective and subjective fact-finding won't be enough. That's why they allow historical performance data to take on more importance than it should.

Past performance simply should not be the major, or sole, reason you hire a particular manager. Not only is past performance no guarantee of future performance, but also there are good reasons to be skeptical of the performance figures presented to you.

Not surprisingly, a manager will give you numbers that make his/her firm look best. Sometimes the manager will give you composite results of several clients, rather than performance for individual portfolios. If this happens, ask for individual portfolio results for corroboration. Conversely, a manager might give you returns on some individual portfolios because those numbers are higher than the firm's overall performance. In that case, request overall returns. In other words, you need both composite and individual portfolio performance results.

And when you're looking at risk-adjusted returns, you need to know some managers calculate their return vs. risk with a geometric mean, and others do so with an arithmetic mean. You want everyone to put it in arithmetic terms.

In addition, make sure you get performance figures on individual portfolios that most closely resemble the kind of portfolio the firm will be managing for you, both in terms of size and investment styles and objectives. If you're considering placing assets in a bank or insurance company commingled fund, don't settle for separate account performance results; make sure you see data for the commingled fund. Naturally, the reverse is also true. In both cases, there's no guarantee the firm manages its commingled fund and separate accounts identically. (Banks and insurers offer commingled, or pooled, funds to clients whose accounts are too small to justify the individual attention of a portfolio manager. Fees usually are lower than for separate account management.)

Be aware of the starting and ending dates managers choose for measurement. A manager's results can change simply by adding or subtracting a year from either the beginning or the end of the period of measurement. Manager A, like other firms, gives you five-year performance numbers. But instead of ending the measurement period in the latest calendar year, Manager A ends the period a year earlier. That's a clue the firm's results for the latest calendar year weren't so hot. In particular, be skeptical of results that start at odd times, such as dates that don't coincide with beginnings and endings of quarters. The four quarters are Jan. 1-March 31; April 1-June 30; July 1-Sept. 30; and Oct. 1-Dec. 31.

Performance data supplied by managers usually will be for three-, five- and 10-year periods. These longer periods can smooth out mistakes managers made in individual years or during market cycles. Obtain quarterly, yearly and market cycle numbers as well. Quarterly numbers will show the portfolio's ups and downs more readily than longer periods will.

Without results for shorter periods, it's too easy for a manager to mask any bad periods. For example, a New Jersey bank was in the top quartile (the top 25% of managers) in *Pensions & Investments Performance Evaluation Report* (*PIPER*) for the five- and 10-year periods for many years. Without quarterly and annual numbers, an investor had no way of knowing the numbers were high only because it was out of the market when it sank in July 1973, yet still was sitting in cash in 1976. Indeed, two good years kept the bank in the top quartile for performance for six or seven years straight.

You also must decide just how many years of performance you want to see. Some investors look at three- and five-year performance records, but with no industry standards regulating managers, there's no way of knowing whether Manager A actually had the same portfolios for those three and five years. Others look at a manager's results over a complete market cycle, that is, from the beginning of one bull market to the beginning of the next, or the beginning of one bear market to the beginning of the next. In this way, they see how a manager performs under a variety of market conditions.

Also, consultants debate the merits of examining results for specific accounts versus all accounts. But most agree a manager's returns should be measured not just against a broad benchmark (such as the Standard & Poor's 500 stock index for equities or the Shearson Lehman Government/Corporate bond index for fixed income) but against a universe or index of the firm's peers. Comparing a growth stock manager's returns with those of the S&P 500, a universe of the largest stocks, wouldn't tell you how good of a growth stock manager he or she is. A consultant could build such benchmarks for you, or might already have them.

A consultant is especially useful for performance evaluation because part of a consultant's stock in trade is to collect performance data from a broad universe of managers. If relying on the managers' own numbers, require some corroboration of performance data. That could include policy decisions that produced the results (something possible, but not easy, for a manager to provide) and corroboration of composite performance data with individual portfolios under management. Some firms offer audited performance data. If so, talk to the auditor to determine the scope of the audit: Did the auditor see all of the firm's accounts or is the auditor merely certifying the accuracy of the accounts he saw?

Face it, no one knowingly hires an investment manager whose investment performance is poor. The point is, performance is but one of many criteria that should be used to evaluate managers. Turn to Step 6 for more details on measuring and monitoring performance.

Hiring a manager solely because of good performance numbers could mean you didn't dig behind the numbers. Perhaps your manager outperformed the Standard & Poor's 500 stock index by several percentage points by buying more speculative stocks than you are willing to own. Examine the risk and reward (or return) relationship too, which is explained in Step 2.

Remember, you'll come across some average managers whose recent numbers are pretty good, and some terrific managers whose recent past performance isn't so good. Your job, made easier with the help of a consultant, is to figure out which is which.

Mistake #2: The firm is hot.

Another way of looking at this mistake is buying a manager high and selling a manager low. Yes, we're repeating ourselves, but there's no guarantee that today's star still will be shining brightly next quarter or next year. Indeed, piles of investment research show the capital markets are cyclical and, therefore, an investment style out of favor now likely will produce handsome returns some time in the future. And given the long-term nature of pension funds, endowments, foundations and other institutions, flash-in-the-pan results aren't necessary.

Institutional investors long have been branded as lemmings and possessed of a herd mentality. Don't be known as one of the crowd that chases the hot item and gets in at the peak. Ask yourself, "Does this manager style really fit into my overall game plan?"

Another way to approach hot managers is to remember that if something sounds too good to be true, it probably is. If history shows 9% or 10% average returns for stocks, why would you believe a manager who promises you long-term results of 25%? Think about it: If they could consistently produce such incredible returns, they probably wouldn't need your business— or anyone else's for that matter; they could retire to some lush tropical isle and merely invest their own money and live off the proceeds.

Some say the leading investment management consulting firms are partly to blame for this lemming-like behavior. Larger consulting firms often don't "discover" a hot manager until the firm has a substantial asset base. That's because many consultants require several years of performance and a minimum amount of assets under management before they will include the manager in their search universe. If you subscribe to the theory that size has a negative effect on performance, then many consultants don't latch on to the hottest managers until after they've peaked.

Mistake #3:   The firm's client contact is attentive and persistent.

We're glad the man or woman with whom you deal makes you feel special. But that person probably won't be managing your portfolio, and is paid to lure clients, not to invest their money. You're not hiring a firm for its marketing expertise—which is what the client contact has—but rather for its investment expertise.

Although the industry, thankfully, has progressed past the point where investors hire the money management firm that does the best job of wining and dining the trustees, some people still get caught up in that. Don't be one of them.

Mistake #4:   You choose the firm that made the best presentation.

Again, you're confusing marketing with investment management. Don't turn the manager selection process into a beauty pageant, which is what happens if you base your decision mainly on the 30-minute or one-hour marketing pitch each firm gives. Doing that ensures you hired good salesmanship, not good portfolio management. One of the key factors in choosing a manager is gaining a solid understanding of the firm's investment process. You won't always get that from a presentation.

Mistake #5:   Someone else recommended the firm.

Most trustees, board members, and corporate executives are smart enough to avoid placing too much weight on the recommendations of a member of their golf foursome who has some indirect experience with hiring people for investment management. Still, even if the person has far more investing experience than you do, that doesn't mean that a manager that's right for his investment needs will do right by you. Perhaps the other guy hired the firm as a bond manager, but you want an equity manager. The manager could have a consistent, winning approach to bonds yet have little or no expertise in stocks. Why, then, would you want that firm as your stock manager?

Investment objectives come into play here as well: Perhaps the other fund has fewer liabilities because of a disproportionately large number of active participants, and your plan is more mature and needs more income and cash flow. As we discussed in Step 2, your investment needs—and therefore your choice of managers—likely are dramatically different from the other guy's.

Mistake #6: You hire a firm with whom you have another relationship.

Too many middle-market investors hire firms with whom they have other business dealings, perhaps their insurance company or bank. Your confidence in that institution likely is based on its primary line of business, which is how you came to have a relationship with it in the first place. Just because a firm is good at handling your health insurance doesn't mean it will be good at handling your investments. Hire your managers based on their investment ability, not their abilities in other businesses.

Mistake #7: The adviser will manage all of your assets.

What a relief! The manager will make all the asset allocation decisions, right? That shouldn't be his or her job. That decision is yours to make, although the advice of investment professionals such as a consultant or manager certainly is warranted. You simply don't hand over all of your money and allow someone else to decide whether to (and how much to) invest in stocks, bonds, real estate or international securities. Those decisions are made before you begin to screen potential money managers. Even a balanced manager, who invests in several asset classes instead of just, say, stocks or bonds, should have guidelines from you, guidelines that still offer the manager discretion, of course. When in doubt, reread Step 3.

Mistake #8: You don't consider the benefits of hiring more than one manager.

No consensus exists on whether to have more than one money manager and on how much you should have in assets before you consider hiring a second one. The time to consider hiring more than one manager is when you begin to question your level of comfort with having all of your investment eggs in one basket. Certainly, you must take pension law into account (the Employee Retirement

Income Security Act of 1974 requires you, as a fiduciary, to act prudently).

If it's diversification you're seeking, be aware you don't guarantee diversification simply by hiring a second manager. Each could be a clone of the other, following the same investment style and buying many of the same securities. The purpose of diversification is to add value either by increasing return or reducing risk; the managers should complement each other. "We're good at what we do," one money manager told us, "but, let's face it, everyone in the business—including our firm—will fall out of favor or make a mistake picking stocks or industries. I wouldn't put all of my money with my firm, so why should a client?"

Some investors believe they create a "horse race" by having two or more managers. There's a problem with that philosophy: Your goal is for all of your managers to achieve your investment objectives, so you want all of them to be winners. In a horse race, there's always a loser. A better way to view this is that hiring a second manager is a safety valve, even if both are core balanced or defensive managers.

Some investment professionals advise waiting until you have at least $10 million before hiring more than one manager. If you divide your assets equally among two managers who give a break in fees at the $5 million level, you'll end up paying the highest fees to both. Many professionals believe investors should shy away from multiple managers if adding a manager will increase costs significantly. That's because managers reduce their fees as the size of an account increases.

But others suggest diversifying by manager style even for those investors with less money; they say you can use mutual funds or commingled funds until you have enough to warrant separate account management.

Sometimes, you eliminate potentially attractive managers by dividing your assets among several managers; some firms have minimum account sizes of $20 million and many have minimums of at least $5 million.

As to whether to add a second balanced manager or to move to specialty managers, part of the answer depends on how involved the investment committee wants to be. Balanced managers are more appropriate for those who don't want to be intimately involved in the asset allocation process because balanced managers require less direction than managers that invest in only one asset class.

We don't want you to feel you must add managers as long as you're happy with the way your account is being run. The expression, "If it ain't broke, don't fix it," applies to investment management too.

Some investment pros say you need $50 million or more in total assets before you begin diversifying into niche or non-core managers, compared with less than half that amount to add balanced or core managers. That's because you probably don't want to put a large percentage of your assets into, say, real estate, venture capital or emerging growth stocks, yet you need enough dollars to qualify for minimum account sizes and to make a difference in meeting your risk and return objectives. If you want separate account management in these specialty areas, you probably will need to give the manager a minimum of $5 million, which would be 10% of a $50 million asset base.

Mistake #9: The firm's fees are less.

Too much weight sometimes is given to fees. You know the trite expressions—you get what you pay for; there's no such thing as a free lunch—and you know there's a ring of truth to them.

Often, there are legitimate reasons why one firm's fees are higher than another's. Perhaps the lower fee is for passive management and the higher one for active management. Perhaps the lower fee is for investing your assets in a commingled fund and the higher one, for investing your assets in a separate account. As Charles C. Field, vice president of money managers Lowe, Brockenbrough, Tierney & Tattersall says, "What you save on fees, you may lose on long-term performance. It doesn't matter how little or how much we charge. If you don't believe we can add more value than the cost of our fee, you shouldn't hire us."

The point is, make sure you don't select a money manager simply because his or her fees appear to be the cheapest around.

Tips On Hiring Money Managers

Knowing what not to do is a start, but it isn't enough. You also must know what to look for.

Roger Bransford, national director of asset consulting for TPF&C admits: "I've been picking managers for 15 years. I can't guarantee I'll pick them any better than you can. I can eliminate them better, but I can't pick them better." Not surprisingly, Bransford believes investors spend far too much time on manager selection, turning the process into a beauty contest when they should simply be looking for a reasonably consistent return that fits in with their risk profile and for a low correlation between and among managers.

In some ways, choosing a manager is no different from choosing a friend or a spouse or an employee. In all cases, you're building relationships, a time-consuming process that is more of an art than a science. First and foremost, many pension executives say, they hire people they feel they know and with whom they are comfortable. For them, competitive performance numbers are important, but less so than their comfort level. "It's really a trust relationship," adds Gary Pines, a principal with TPF&C. "The difficulty in hiring a manager is building a new relationship."

Discussions with many investors prove Charles Ellis was on the right track when he said in his book, *Investment Policy*, that among the criteria for manager selection are professional investment competence; commitment to client service; and soundness of business strategy. You also must have a clear concept of how the firm will add value to your portfolio. You must understand the investment process, such as how the firm selects its investments, how it determines which securities offer superior returns and how it decides when to sell a security. And, of course, the firm must have a valid record of achievement.

But there are a number of steps to take before you're ready to hire a money manager.

Manager selection involves planning, obtaining basic information, interviewing, selecting and formalizing, says Duncan Smith, senior vice president-manager research, for Frank Russell Co. in Tacoma, Washington. In a 1988 commentary, "How to Select and Evaluate

Investment Managers," Smith contends most investors concentrate on the interviewing component, yet most errors in manager selection result from deficiencies in the other stages.

Stage 1: Deciding what types of managers, and how many of each, you want.

The planning is done during the investment policy and asset allocation stages, which we addressed in Steps 2 and 3. Since studies suggest only about 7% of total portfolio returns reflect stock selection, the selection of portfolio managers should be driven by the asset allocation process, rather than the asset allocation process being driven by the managers. Having made your asset allocation decisions, you'll be able to set up criteria to help whittle down the number of potential candidates, such as types of managers you want to hire (stock, bond, real estate, international, balanced, short term and the like); number of managers per asset class; active vs. passive management; size of portfolio to be managed by each manager; and range of fees you're willing to pay.

We can't give you any formula for determining what kind of manager to hire; indeed, every investment professional has his or her own ideas. One consultant recommends an investor with $20 million should hire one low-risk manager and one more aggressive manager, while another consultant suggests that same investor should tap a stock manager, a bond manager and a manager that specializes in guaranteed investment contracts (as a way to reduce risk). Basically, there are as many suggestions and combinations as there are people to make them.

Stage 2: Gathering basic information about the likely candidates.

Once you've settled on the kinds of managers you're hiring, here is some basic information you'll want to gather prior to interviews:

- History of the firm and background of the key staffers (especially those who would be involved in managing your portfolio);

- Minimum and maximum account sizes accepted as well as the total assets under management and number of clients;

- Breadth and depth of the staff's experience in portfolio management, research, marketing, trading and operations;

- Ownership of the company;

- Number of accounts per portfolio manager;

- Investment philosophy and investment style;

- Structure of the firm's decision-making process;

- Source of its research (how much is internally generated vs. bought from other sources);

- Stability of the professional staff;

- Fees;

- Operational capability;

- Compensation structure for key personnel (especially those assigned to your portfolio).

Clients of many consultants answer a series of questions dealing with their expectations of a manager, which helps the consultant choose which managers to include in the search. One question might be whether the client wants to direct brokerage, meaning whether he or she wants to hire money managers that will direct a portion of their transactions to specific brokerage firms. That way, the client can pay part or all of the consultant's fees in soft dollars (rather than in cash, or hard dollars). Many, but not all, money managers will direct brokerage, as long as the commissions are used to pay for value-added services.

Another question is whether trustees would be comfortable with having a client service specialist, rather than a portfolio manager, as their primary contact. If trustees insist on dealing exclusively with a portfolio manager, that eliminates a number of firms.

Establishing criteria sometimes can cause an unexpected headache: One consultant said trustees at a public pension fund recently came up with seven requirements for new managers they were evaluating, yet none of their existing managers could meet the criteria. What should they do? Should they adhere to their criteria or alter the criteria to accommodate the firms with which they have existing relationships?

Stage 3:   Establishing criteria for the size of the firm.

Don't wait for the interview process to decide such basic require- ments as the size of the firm you would consider. One manager tells of being weeded out of a search after making a presentation because his firm was too small. Both the committee and the manager wasted time and energy in a situation that could have been avoided had the size criterion been set earlier. The same is true of a geographic bias.

Stage 4:   Gathering sample client reports and checking references.

Also ahead of time, you'll want sample reports. And don't forget client references. Be sure to check with former as well as existing clients.

Use the references you're given. "People give you high-profile references, thinking you'll never call them," believes consultant Bill Wurts. And don't be afraid to call other sources in addition to the list of references.

Stage 5:   Examining performance data.

And, finally, you'll want performance numbers—time-weighted— for the periods ending with the most recent quarter. Look at quarter-by-quarter returns, unannualized returns for each year, and compounded annual returns for longer periods such as three, five and 10 years.

One giant caveat: Managers have a way of massaging their data or manipulating statistics so they all show up in the top quartile (the highest 25%) when compared against other managers. They'll do so, for example, by giving you dollar-weighted composite returns during a bear market, with the composite dominated by a large, conservative public pension fund that had no more than 30% in equities. A new firm that started during a period that was bad for its management style could give its record during a time it was heavily invested in cash equivalents while it was waiting to invest new client money. A start-up firm also could string together a composite of two partners' performance at other companies, taking the best years for each of them. Even an established firm might pick one of its 50 accounts to showcase. Or, if it's a bull market, the firm could tell you how well its stocks did, without mentioning its bonds didn't fare as well.

Carefully scrutinize manager-supplied data; performance data obtained from a consultant or performance measurement service can be more valid. Check the validity of performance reports that managers tell you come from consultants. Sometimes those reports haven't been prepared by consultants at all. In some cases, managers get hold of consultant report sheets and insert their own data. The ins and outs of performance are explored in Step 6.

Talk about performance with the manager's references. While you have the reference on the phone, compare the performance numbers you got from the manager with the numbers from the client's own portfolio. If there are differences, discuss those during the manager interview.

Much of the basic data you'll need can be obtained by sending questionnaires to managers, talking to consultants and executives and trustees of other funds and reading industry trade publications, such as *Pensions & Investments* and *Institutional Investor*.

Stage 6: Conducting and managing the interviews.

Once you've gathered all the preliminary information and have weighed and analyzed that data, you're ready to choose candidates to interview and to conduct—and manage—the interviews. And "interview" or "dialogue" would be the operative word here, not "presentation." You don't want to be sold, you want to interview and be interviewed. You want a dialogue. This is a forum through which you and the money manager determine whether you are well-suited to work together.

Any question is fair game. If you're a corporate financial officer, you wouldn't want a vendor to ask you, "How are you compensated?" But that's a legitimate question to ask of a manager. One of the manager's goals should be to convince you that the money management business is a business just like yours. You need to get to know the manager on a business level, not as if there's a mystique that doesn't exist in the normal business world.

Most trustees or investment committees conduct these face-to-face meetings in their own offices. That's certainly acceptable and understandable, given financial and time restraints. But Jack Marco, head of Jack Marco Consulting Group, tells of one Taft-Hartley fund client that insisted on interviewing each manager on his own turf. Over a six-month period, trustees visited more than 30 managers, each for half a day. This way, he recalls, they were able to meet not just the chief investment officer and the marketing person, but also analysts, operations people and all of the portfolio managers and support staffers. "The investment management process is 90% people," he says, and seeing those people in action is revealing.

Just as you obtained quantitative information through questionnaires, so will you obtain qualitative information through interviews. Both are necessary for an intelligent selection.

Although there's no rule on how many firms to interview, the range seems to be three to four, selected from an initial group about twice as large. Expect each interview to take at least an hour, although Field says: "If we can't explain in a half hour what we do, then we don't know it well enough to explain it." Prepare and organize for the interviews by listing the goals to be accomplished and the issues to be raised. Sending the candidates that same list will help them gear their presentation to your needs, and will reduce the amount of time spent on traditional marketing pitches.

Stage 7: Selecting questions to ask the candidates.

Don't hesitate to focus on the people aspect. Get a feel for how the people interact and whether they have a shared, but streamlined, decision-making process. Ask them about the single most difficult aspect of running their firm. Ask how you can hold them accountable.

In his commentary, Frank Russell's Duncan Smith recommends knowing who is responsible for such key decisions as establishing the level and timing of cash reserves; deciding the emphasis to be placed on themes, sectors and industries; determining which stocks are to be purchased and sold; developing the actual portfolio; and reviewing portfolio results.

Dig into the background of the staff. Newer firms might oversell the backgrounds of the key staffers while they were at other companies because the firm itself won't have a track record.

Quiz each candidate about his or her investment style: When does the firm do well in a market cycle? When doesn't it? You could take this approach one step further, asking the candidate what actions he or she takes when the market moves against the firm's style. "Remember, you're not buying widgets—a one-time product—so you have to understand how the investment product is produced," advises consultant Jack Marco. Otherwise, you could be shaken out when a manager's style is out of favor.

Understanding the investment process is crucial. Many consultants reject the notion of a so-called "black box" method of investing that is so quantitative or laden with sophisticated, proprietary computer systems that only a rocket scientist could understand it. "I don't think there should ever be a black box," suggests TPF&C's Gary Pines. With that kind of process, the manager is implying, "Trust me." And there are enough good managers out there that an investor needn't give blind trust to anyone.

Part of understanding the investment process requires an assessment of risk at the portfolio level. Among the considerations: How is diversification used? How often are strategic changes made? How does the manager decide which risks are appropriate to take? We tackled risk in Step 2.

Also get a handle on how your portfolio would be structured. With an equity manager, for example, you will want to know the capitalization, price/earnings ratio, price/book ratio, beta, yield, earnings growth and other characteristics of a typical stock in the portfolio. It will show you whether he or she is following the promised style.

AMR Investment Services' Bill Quinn has hired dozens of money managers as head of the American Airlines employee benefit funds. He always looks for "people with disciplines who follow them, and have a good, stable management team. That means sometimes you're boring, you're not in the latest fad, but it works."

Summing Up

Finding someone to help you reach your investment goals isn't as simple as just hiring a manager with good performance numbers. You'll have to contend with objective and subjective information. The objective information will be based on the past achievements of the manager and on your own risk and return goals. The subjective part, the elements of judgment, will be based on which managers you think are likely to be future achievers and, as importantly, which managers best meet your needs.

Here are some questions as you go through the manager evaluation and selection process:

1. What kind of and how many managers do I want?
2. Have I gathered as much information as possible on each candidate prior to the interview? Refer to Step 2 for the detailed information you're seeking.
3. Have I seen reports the firm prepares for other clients?
4. Have I checked references?
5. Do I understand the firm's historical performance record? If I obtained that information from that firm, have I corroborated it independently?
6. Have I prepared an agenda for the interviews and sent it to each candidate?

7. Have I prepared a list of pertinent questions for each manager?

8. Do I have a clear understanding of the investment philosophy of each firm?

STEP 6

STEP 6:

Staying On Target

*"Even if you're on the right track, you'll get
run over if you just stand still."*
WILL ROGERS

If you want to stay on target, you've got to monitor performance on an ongoing basis.

Still, many investment pros believe the emphasis on performance (or how your portfolio stacks up against an arbitrary benchmark like the Standard & Poor's 500 stock index or against a universe of other managed portfolios) has gotten out of hand. No one is sure who's to blame; most likely, it's some combination of everyone involved, including investors, consultants and money managers.

Some good has come out of this emphasis on performance. No longer are most institutional investors thought to be passive followers of a buy-and-hold strategy. Some observers laud investors' shorter time horizons: They thought it was unrealistic for pension executives, for example, to invest for 20 or 30 years into the future when the executives wouldn't be around to reap the rewards or suffer the consequences of their investment decisions.

And money managers seem to work harder for their fees these days.

The flip side, however, is the concern that investors are becoming too short-sighted. Almost everyone is trying to be, or trying to find, today's hot manager. When asked what will happen if today's winning manager turns out to be tomorrow's loser, some investors sound like Scarlett O'Hara. "I'll worry about that tomorrow," they say.

Many consulting firms reinforce this emphasis on performance in their client reports. How a client's managers performed often is the first section in the report. At least one firm—the consulting arm of Merrill Lynch—is moving manager rankings further back in the report and putting information on how much money the client earned up front.

Throughout this book, we've tried to put performance in its proper perspective, that of a report card that grades not just the money manager, but everyone connected with the management of the assets. Now, you'll learn how to measure and evaluate performance results. At the same time, you'll catch a glimpse of the common performance measurement mistakes and how to avoid them.

First, measure the performance of the fund as a whole against your stated goal. What has been the total return of the fund over one, three and five years? How close is that to the long-term target rate of return? Was this return achieved within the risk guidelines set in the investment policy statement? If the fund has outperformed its target, should the target be changed? Was it too conservative or are the results an anomaly? Should the risk guidelines now be changed? Can the fund now adopt a lower risk, lower return investment policy? Should it? If you have multiple managers, once you have examined the performance of the total portfolio, you then can examine the performance of each manager.

If you have a pension fund, separate your review of the relative performance of your money managers from your review of whether the fund is meeting the actuarial and investment objectives you've established. Your review should include not just whether the managers achieved the desired rate of return, but also whether the sponsor's contribution and funded status targets were met. Don't just look at the portfolio's rate of return, your manager's ranking in some universe and how a benchmark did. Determine how many dollars your portfolio earned and whether you now have enough money to meet your liabilities and if you met your actuary's interest-rate assumption and your own rate-of-return assumption. Remember the raw numbers aren't risk adjusted, and you (with the help of your consultant) need to measure your manager's returns in relation to how much risk the firm took to achieve those results.

Most mistakes are made when it comes to how, and against what, you measure performance.

Mistake #1:   Measuring a manager's performance against inappropriate benchmarks.

In the lingo of investment management, benchmark buzzwords are essential. It's OK to measure your manager or your portfolio against the passive indexes—the Standard & Poor's 500 stock index for equities; the Shearson Lehman Government/Corporate bond index or the Salomon Broad Investment Grade index for fixed income; Donoghue's Money Market index for cash; the FRC Property Index for real estate; and the Morgan Stanley Capital International Europe Australia Far East index for international. But it's not good to use them as the only yardsticks against which all investment managers should be measured.

Say you've hired a balanced manager, giving him/her discretion to move among stocks, bonds and cash, with few strings attached. Say that manager was prescient enough to move out of stocks during the third quarter of 1987 (the period ended Sept. 30), thus minimizing the effects of the stock market meltdown in October. It would be just plain unfair to measure your balanced portfolio against the S&P 500 for the quarter ended Sept. 30, when the stock market was still rising. If you did so, your manager wouldn't look good, even though you both know he was a hero. In fact, a balanced account should never be measured against the S&P 500, but against a composite index of stocks, bonds and cash, and against other balanced managers.

On the fixed-income side, you would be doing yourself a disservice by agreeing to take substantially more risk and hiring a high-yield (or junk bond) manager, then measuring the junk bond portfolio against the Shearson Lehman or the Salomon Broad Investment Grade indexes. In this case, your junk bond manager might look terrific compared to the index. But if you measure your manager against a universe of other junk bond managers, you might discover your manager's performance lagged, even though your manager took as many risks as the better performing managers.

Similarly, if the needs of your fund dictate investing in a portfolio with bond maturities of between six and eight years, it would be unfair to measure your fixed-income portfolio against only the longer-term Shearson Lehman Government/Corporate index (which had about a 9 1/2-year maturity when this book was written) or that firm's intermediate index (which had an average maturity of about 4.1 years). If you use a blended index (by measuring your portfolio against 50% of the return of each of those indexes), you'll wind up with a maturity of slightly close to seven years. That's smack dab in the middle of the maturities of your portfolio.

Use the indexes, but blend them proportionately to match the composition of your portfolio. If you restrict your balanced manager to a specific asset allocation mix, measure the account against the indexes in the same proportions. That means for an account with a 40% allocation to bonds and a 60% allocation to stocks, the bond return should be measured against 40% of the return of the Shearson Lehman or Salomon bond indexes or another appropriate benchmark, and the stock return should be measured against 60% of the return of the S&P 500 or another appropriate index. When measuring the performance of a balanced manager's portfolio against indexes, some consultants include in their blended index 10% of the return on Treasury bills, since balanced managers often hold 10% of assets in cash.

If you give your balanced manager discretion to move between stocks and bonds, start by measuring the returns of your portfolio against 50% of the return of a stock index and 50% of the return of a bond index. You should expect your manager's return to be better than that 50/50 return, however, because you gave the manager permission to vary the asset allocation in hopes of adding value.

The key is to sectionalize portfolios and measure the right proportion of the portfolio against the proper universe and the right proportion of an index.

Don't agree to use general yardsticks because your money managers favor them. Most managers are only too happy to sign off on traditional benchmarks against which you'll measure them. That's because the overall plan's benchmarks probably will be easier to reach than specific benchmarks. So, set specific benchmarks for each manager, which should be jointly agreed upon, in writing, by you and the manager. A consultant can help you establish appropriate benchmarks for each manager.

Mistake #2:   Ignoring your goals and objectives when measuring performance.

No manager can consistently lead the pack in an up market and preserve your assets in a down market, and you couldn't realistically have both objectives in your policy statement. Why, then, would you expect your portfolio to be a top performer in both a bull and a bear market?

Don't be blind to your investment objectives. If preservation of capital was high on your goals, don't get angry at your manager's returns in a bull market if your portfolio trails the market averages. If the manager is doing what you hired him/her to do, your portfolio probably won't be in the top decile (10%) and might not be in the top quartile (25%). And that's OK.

Money managers complain that investors only give lip service to the concept of looking beyond performance numbers to find out how the fund is doing. Instead of saying, "Here's what I needed and here's what I got," many investors see that another manager had higher numbers than their manager did, and they get angry. Consultant Bob Padgette, president of the Mobius Group, Inc., believes it's foolhardy for investors to lose sight of what they expect to accomplish and to emphasize the universe comparisons. "They figure if they're OK relative to everybody else, that'll be good enough," he says. "But if you were in the steel business in 1981 and you happened to be the best steel company, that only meant you were going broke less quickly. It doesn't really mean anything."

Mistake #3: Looking at returns that are not adjusted for risk.

Just as you must understand the relationship between risk and return to make informed and prudent investment decisions, so must you understand the relationship in order to properly evaluate your managers. Many consultants use a risk-return graph to show the concept that there's a reason for a high rate of return—you take more risk.

To construct the graph, or risk-return matrix, you need 12 to 20 quarters (or three to five years) of historical performance data.

Study the illustration on page 107, and note that the matrix plots annualized return versus the volatility of the portfolio (expressed as standard deviation, which measures the absolute volatility of each quarterly return around a certain mean return). The vertical axis measures the portfolio's return, the horizontal axis measures risk.

The matrix forms four quadrants, where the horizontal and vertical lines intersect at the risk-return point for the Standard & Poor's 500 stock index. The northwest quadrant (the upper left quarter of the matrix) represents high return/low risk; the northeast quadrant, high return/high risk; the southwest quadrant, low return/low risk; and the southeast quadrant, low return/high risk.

Then, after plotting the returns on the matrix from Treasury bills and the stock market, draw a line connecting the two. That line is the capital market line, a theoretical line representing investments without market risk (T-bills) and investments with inherent market risk (S&P 500 stocks). Investment theory says that as investors assume more risk, they should be rewarded with a higher rate of return. That's why the capital market line slopes upward. High returns seldom come without a good dose of risk: That's why you must set risk parameters for your managers, as we explained in Step 2, and why you must monitor the managers' adherence to those parameters as part of measuring their performance.

Mistake #4: Suffering from "QP."

"QP"—quarterly paranoia—"is the absolute enemy of this business, and we (consultants) invented it," frets John L. Kornet Jr., president

RISK REWARD MATRIX

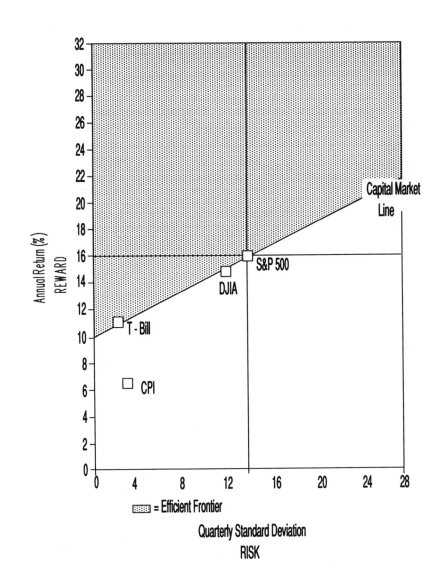

Source: Shearson Lehman Hutton

of Global Perspectives, Inc. Why? "Because we needed something to sell."

Kornet contends the obsession with quarterly performance figures is the "single most destructive force in our business... everyone has lost sight of the big picture."

Thomas E. Johnson, president of Tom Johnson Investment Management, remembers a recent conversation he had with a competitor. "We started talking about quarters, but ended up talking about months. I was talking about our performance in October when we were only four or five trading days into the month."

Two other incidents along these same lines cropped up in the course of researching this book. Once, at a cocktail party, two portfolio managers were comparing their years to date, through Sept. 30. When they finished, one said to the other, "Yeah, but how did you do this month?" The other started to respond, then interrupted himself, saying, "Wait a minute, the month isn't over yet." Another time, a consultant was considering marriage. "We'll make a decision in the first quarter," he said.

Mistake #5:   Ignoring important checks and balances.

Sometimes a manager or a master trustee makes a mistake in reporting performance. One of the important roles of the consultant is to spot that mistake. The consultant's job also is to provide you with data on performance, so you don't have to rely solely on the manager's numbers. The consultant, then, functions as part of a checks and balances system.

Mistake #6:   Excluding cash when measuring performance.

Unless the manager has 100% of your assets in the investment class you hired him/her to invest in, some of your money is in cash or cash equivalents. Insist on including cash when measuring performance, because that cash is part of the total assets available for investment. In a bull market, cash will lower the overall returns; in a bear market, cash will increase them.

The effect of cash ón returns can be dramatic. Mike Clowes, editor of *Pensions & Investments*, tells of a California money manager who was puzzled about a comparison of his returns and those of a competitor. The manager asked Clowes whether there was any way he and his competitor could have different returns when they began and ended the measurement period with the same amount of money. Each was given $10 million, and each ended up with $12 million, yet one was up 20% and the other claimed to be up 33%. After much deliberation, Clowes figured it out: The high-performing manager only measured the performance of his stocks; he excluded his cash returns, those from short-term cash equivalents. Of course, since he made the decision to go to cash, the cash returns, which were lower than the stock returns, should have been included. This would have lowered his overall return.

Mistake #7:   Having overly high expectations of the value of performance measurement.

As we keep insisting, there are lots of wrong ways to look at performance measurement. One right and simple way to regard it is as a report card. One reason schools require students to get their parents' signatures on report cards is to guarantee the parent an opportunity to view the child's progress, as measured by grades. Similarly, performance results can be a forced means of getting you to look at and discuss your investments and your investment needs. Trustees should discuss performance of their managers and of the fund in relation to actuarial and investment needs among themselves.

Whenever possible, give the performance report to the manager before you meet with him or her. That way, the meeting will focus on the investment process, not on the actual numbers. You also don't want to waste time listening to your managers complain that they were measured incorrectly. If they see their performance numbers in advance, they can argue their merits in advance as well. If you employ a consultant, he or she can quibble with the manager over the report well before all of you sit down to talk about it.

Look at the manager's total return in comparison with your target return, as set forth in your investment policy statement. See if the manager followed your written investment guidelines, on which he/she should have signed off. Learn how the manager contributed to the achievement of your overall investment objectives, remembering the objectives are for the overall fund, not just for one manager. If the manager's performance was poor, perhaps it is the fault of your investment policy.

Indeed, evaluating manager performance often leads to a reexamination of the fund's investment policies. Determine if the manager followed the investment approach he/she said would be used. One example often cited by both managers and consultants is that of value managers, many of whom take up to three years to begin adding value through their purchase of out-of-favor stocks. If you hired a value manager, you shouldn't necessarily be alarmed at his performance after a year or two. Or, if you hired a small-capitalization stock manager in the mid-1980s, and the firm's performance has been below that of your other managers but on par with or better than other small-cap managers, you might want to focus on whether you should continue to emphasize small-cap stocks, rather than focus on that manager's performance.

Some investment pros complain that middle-market investors sometimes expect instant results. Says money manager Gary P. Brinson, of Brinson Partners: "The worst thing that happens to a middle-market investor is he takes the corporate mentality, which is great for the production business, and applies it to the investment business, where it doesn't work." If the quality or quantity of production on an assembly line slips, Brinson notes, company executives know they have a problem, so they tell the foreman, "Fix it, it's broken." They monitor investment performance the same way: "If it's slipping, they call in the manager and tell him to fix it. But in the investment business, nothing may be broken; it's just the nature of markets and market cycles." The worst offenders are executives in the retailing industry, Brinson says. "They have the worst mentality. They get weekly sales reports in their business, so they expect weekly reports on the performance of their portfolios."

Mistake #8: Not knowing how to calculate and evaluate performance.

You'll want to get time-weighted returns from your managers, not dollar-weighted. The difference? Time-weighted returns measure the performance of the money manager; dollar-weighted returns measure the performance of the fund.

That's because time-weighted numbers minimize the effects of cash flows, such as additional contributions—which managers generally don't control—to and from a portfolio; dollar-weighted figures measure returns attributable to the timing or size of cash flows. The only time they are identical is when there are no cash inflows or outflows or when the return earned during the period is constant.

More specifically, time-weighted returns show the value of $1 invested for the entire period; they are calculated by measuring the return during sub-periods (such as quarters), with interim returns chained or linked. They separate the impact of contributions and disbursements from returns generated by the investment process, but require a market valuation of the portfolio at the time a contribution or disbursement occurs.

Dollar-weighted returns show the average return of all the dollars invested for the period. They reduce to zero the value of cash flows and capital appreciation or depreciation minus the starting assets. They assume cash flows are within control of the investment manager, which isn't always true.

Time-weighted rates of return have their problems, of course. You have to decide, for example, when to calculate the return, especially when short-term investments are actively traded. Ideally, returns should not be calculated for securities in the portfolio that haven't been held throughout the measurement period. That's easier said than done: Those who make their living by providing performance measurement data are loathe to report no results at all for some segments of portfolios they monitor.

Once you've mastered timed-weighted rates of return, calculate the total return, not yield or any other one factor alone. Total return includes realized income from dividends plus interest payments as well as realized and unrealized market gains or losses.

Whenever possible, subtract fees from that total. Many performance measurement firms don't subtract out certain costs (including, sometimes, the investment management fee or the master trust fee) because the costs aren't reported to them. Many consultants obtain the data from investors' custodial or master trust banks, then reenter it into their computers. But the banks might not have subtracted out fees, either.

You'll want the manager's returns to be net of fees because the index you're comparing him to—such as the S&P 500—is net of fees, and the manager has an unfair advantage over the index if he/she provides gross, not net, numbers. Accounting for investment management fees is especially important if you've hired an index fund manager whose goal is to mirror a specific index. Say you hire an S&P 500 stock index manager, and your indexed portfolio returned 13.2% for a one-year period while the S&P returned 13%. That doesn't mean your portfolio outperformed the index by two-tenths of one percentage point: You paid a fee to the manager to run your indexed assets. Before fees, you outperformed the index by 20 basis points (100 basis points equal one percentage point), so unless you paid 19 basis points or less to the manager, your portfolio's return didn't match the S&P 500's.

Calculate the value of the assets held by the manager at market value, not cost or book value. Public pension funds (state, municipal and other government groups) that manage their assets internally are notorious for calculating their assets at book value, or the price at which they bought them. In a bull market, they're cheating themselves; in a bear market, they're kidding themselves.

Make sure you take risk into account when evaluating your manager's performance. A manager who outshines everyone in his/her category might have taken significant risks to do so. And if the manager continues to employ that strategy in the future, you must be prepared for periods of horrendous performance, too.

Indeed, many consultants believe it is important to look at risk-adjusted rates of return, as is explained in Mistake #3.

Mistake #9: Failing to determine the manager's contribution to performance.

Rate of return is only the first step in determining the manager's contribution to performance. Investors also must determine the reasons for the performance, including asset commitment, selection and redeployment.

A manager could have obtained good returns by having a large equity commitment (since stocks outperform bonds and cash over time), by making superior security selections and/or by making good decisions on how to redeploy, or reinvest, assets. Ronald Surz, a principal with Becker, Burke Associates, calls this "attribution" for who added value and how value is added, or how to measure the skill it took for one manager to outperform another manager.

Consultant George Dunn of Shearson Lehman Hutton uses an experience he had with a client to illustrate the usefulness of determining the manager's contribution to performance. He tells of a $10 million account with a balanced manager that was 50% invested in stocks and 50% invested in bonds. The account returned 14% compounded annually for the five years ended Dec. 31, 1986. When he sectionalized the performance, he found that the fixed-income component returned 19% and the equities, 9%. From that examination, the client decided the manager was far more successful at managing bonds than stocks, so the firm was retained as a fixed-income manager for $5 million, and the other $5 million was split between two new equity specialists in hopes of improving equity performance.

If you're measuring a new manager's contribution, consider waiting at least three months before beginning the measurement cycle. This transition period gives the manager time to set up your portfolio, to invest the cash you have given him and/or to sell any unwanted stocks he/she inherited.

Summing Up

Yes, measuring performance is important because you need to know if you're staying on target. That said, however, here are some questions to review to make sure you put performance measurement in its proper context:

1. What benchmarks am I using to measure my manager against? Do I blend them when appropriate?

2. In addition to comparing my managers' returns to those of the indexes and universes of other managers, am I reviewing performance in relation to my investment goals and actuarial assumptions?

3. Do I understand the relationship between risk and return, and did I properly evaluate the amount of risk the manager took to achieve the returns?

4. When reporting their performance, do my managers include cash? For example, is a stock manager only giving me his equity returns, even if he had 20% of my assets invested in cash?

5. Are the returns net of management fees?

6. Are they time-weighted returns?

7. What is my manager's contribution to the returns?

STEP 7

STEP 7:

Knowing When A Manager Is In Trouble

*"Forget about a return **on** my investment; what I want is a return **of** my investment."*
WILL ROGERS

Don't hold your breath waiting for your money manager to say: "I've done a lousy job, you should fire me." That's up to you to figure out. But by reading this chapter, you'll learn how and why investors often miss the warning signs. Then, we'll tell you how to recognize that your portfolio may be in jeopardy and what to do and not do about it.

Mistake #1:   Missing clues that something is amiss.

Among the more obvious hints:

• Your portfolio was reassigned to another staffer.

Find out why: Did one or more people quit? Did your portfolio manager get a promotion? Did they assign a lower-level person to your account and what does that mean?

- One or more key investment people left the firm.

Such information should be given to clients immediately. If not, you can learn of departures from your investment management consultant, from competing money managers, from trustees and executives of other funds and from regularly reading industry publications that carry such news (including *Pensions & Investments, Money Management Letter* and *Investment Management Weekly*). Once you learn of the defections, dig for the reasons, and determine how this will affect your portfolio.

- Several major clients terminated their accounts with the manager.

You'll learn about this the same way you'll learn of staff departures. Don't panic until you talk to those clients directly (your peers at other funds). Perhaps they restructured their funds and switched from balanced managers to equity and fixed-income specialists, whereas you still want balanced management. Just because the firm is no longer a good fit for other clients doesn't mean it's not the right firm for you.

- Assets under management declined.

Even if the manager hasn't been hit by high account turnover, clients could be reducing their allocations to the firm. Your job is to find out why the firm's assets have decreased, and why its clients are reducing their allocations. The reasons could be logical: Clients with several pension plans terminated one or two liquidating assets in order to buy annuities to pay vested benefits; the firm decided to close its doors to new clients and is not replacing assets lost through normal attrition.

- Assets under management increased dramatically.

That sounds like good news, but it isn't necessarily the case. In effect, the firm has become too successful and may have difficulty digesting its rapid growth. One obvious sign is that operational problems continually crop up. Another is that the key investment staffers are always on the road, making marketing and client service calls instead of staying home managing the money. A third is that individual portfolio managers find themselves overseeing too many accounts. Future investment performance also could suffer if the key decision makers who built the record are forced to bring in second stringers—younger, less experienced portfolio managers—to handle all the new accounts and some of the old ones. Finally, if a firm takes on too much money too fast, it could be forced to change its investment style. This particularly can be a problem for a small, aggressive growth-stock manager who suddenly finds himself managing $400 million to $500 million instead of $50 million, and is forced to greatly expand his universe of stocks and the number of positions he holds.

• Performance slipped.

Again, don't panic. This doesn't necessarily mean the firm has lost its luster. If you hired the firm as a large-capitalization manager, and small-cap stocks suddenly are soaring, it makes sense your manager's results will be less than stellar. Before firing the manager, reexamine your investment policy to determine if you want to stick with a large-cap strategy. Then, compare your manager's performance with that of other large-cap managers to get a better perspective of your manager's returns.

• Communication with your manager breaks down.

A good investment management firm knows it must service existing clients with as much zeal as it exhibits when it recruits new clients. If your manager begins to ignore your phone calls, or you no longer get the level of personal attention you had come to expect, something could be wrong. During bad times, your client contact should be staying in touch with you, letting you know he or she is aware of your concerns. The client contact also should inform you what actions the firm is taking to remedy the problem. If you don't hear from your manager after a day like Oct. 19, 1987, when the market dropped 508 points, ask why.

• Your manager, an equity specialist, suddenly develops an interest in managing fixed-income portfolios.

This could mean the principals know they're in trouble with their current client base. Perhaps they can't market their equity numbers because they are mediocre, so, in an effort to maintain revenue growth, they diversify their product line.

- When the name of the firm changes.

Find out the reason: it might materially affect your decision to stay with the firm. For example, the founder of one Midwest firm got into serious trouble with the Securities and Exchange Commission, changed the name of his firm, and continued to do business. Even today, many consultants and investors aren't aware of the connection between the two firms. Another reason for a name change could be the departure of one or more of the principals and/or owners.

- Ownership of the firm changed.

Many money management firms have changed hands or gone public because the previous owners wanted some liquidity to their net worth. That doesn't mean the firm's method of operation or staff will necessarily change: often the founders remain in their positions following the ownership change. Still, clients should be alert to any ownership changes and should find out what the effects will be. Often the previous owners are bound to the firm for only five years. After that, they might leave to retire or start anew.

- When there is turnover of marketing people.

Marketers know they must have a competitive product to sell and credibility with consultants. Plus, they don't want their reputation to go down with the firm.

Mistake #2:   Failing to recognize inconsistencies.

Consistency of style and approach is a key ingredient to long-term investment success. Simply put, if a manager changes style or approach, watch out. It's a good idea to look continually at the composition of your portfolio, and if anomalies arise (such as a large-cap manager suddenly buying low-quality stocks) don't be afraid to question your manager or your consultant.

William F. Quinn, who oversees the pension fund of American Airlines, remembers one firm he hired that was a regional division of a New York company. When top management changed in New York, the regional office's investment philosophy changed. Before that, the regional office was allowed to pursue its own style. Suddenly, however, the regional division lost its autonomy, and was forced to follow the investment approach of the new management. The result? Quinn terminated the manager.

Managers whose performance begins to lag are key candidates to practice inconsistencies, as though they were changing their approach in a last-ditch effort to catch up. But some investors and consultants will fire a manager even when the firm is doing well if its style changes.

Mistake #3:   Allowing personal involvement to cloud your judgment.

As a fiduciary or trustee, don't let a personal relationship affect your objectivity. Maintaining a friendly, but arms-length relationship is important if you ever find it necessary to dismiss a manager for cause.

Mistake #4:   Arbitrarily giving a manager a set amount of time to perform.

Anyone who ever has asked the question, "How long should I give a manager to perform?" has gotten the standard response: three to five years.

Many investment pros say market cycles, not the calendar, should determine how long to give a manager. But there is much disagreement over how long a market cycle lasts. Take the bull market that began in 1982: Some say that cycle hasn't ended yet because there hasn't been a corresponding bear market; others say the 508-point drop in the market on Oct. 19, 1987, signaled the beginning of the downside of the cycle.

Probably the best idea is to remain flexible, to lengthen or shorten the time period as circumstances warrant. Quinn tells of one manager, "a real contrarian," who didn't do well for the first three or four years he managed money for American. But Quinn hung on and, a couple of years later, "the guy worked out."

Some investors complain (and more than a few money managers agree) that consultants sometimes put pressure on them to hire and fire managers too quickly. It's important to remember you have to give your manager enough time for the firm's investment style to add value. If you hire a manager to be defensive, and he or she returns an average of 15% while the market is up 20% one year and 30% the next year, or an average of 25%, you might be tempted to fire the manager. Think again. The firm likely accomplished your objectives. To protect your assets in a down market, a defensive manager likely will give up something in an up market. Wait until the market favors that manager's investment style before you seal the firm's fate.

Mistake #5:   Basing your decision solely on the numbers.

Even if the manager is turning in strong performance and doing what you hired him or her for, you still might feel uneasy.

That's OK. That's chemistry at work, the same chemistry that is important in any relationship. That chemistry had to be there when you hired the firm, just as it is when two people begin a love relationship. But chemistry changes and fades (witness the nation's divorce rate), and it's OK to be concerned if you just plain don't like the firm, its people, or its approach as much as you once did. You didn't promise an indefinite, no-cut contract. If you know it's not working out, or if for any reason you've lost confidence, replace your manager.

Mistake #6:   Using performance data incorrectly to make your decisions.

No one denies that manager performance is one of the key criteria to use to determine whether to retain or terminate a manager. But professionals sometimes question the kind of data investors use and how they use that data.

For example, you shouldn't necessarily terminate an equity manager because his returns have been lower than the Standard &

Poor's 500 stock index over the last 12 to 18 months. Perhaps he's a small-cap manager. If the S&P 500—which measures the market's largest capitalized companies—is doing well, that might be just an indication your manager's style has been out of favor.

Even with a tailored benchmark, you have to decide how far off the mark the manager must be before you fire him or her. One consultant said if everything else was OK, he wouldn't recommend terminating a manager unless the firm missed its benchmark by more than 300 basis points (or three percentage points, since 100 basis points equal one percentage point) for more than one year. Even then, evaluate the manager's returns thoroughly. Perhaps on a risk-adjusted basis, the returns look better.

And don't confuse bad luck with bad strategy. One year of poor performance could mean only that the manager's timing was a little off, that he or she was too early in making a move that later will be considered brilliant. The strategy could prove sound if you give it some time to work out.

Mistake #7:   Changing managers too often.

Just as it's possible to ignore signs of trouble and, thus, allow a poorly performing manager to continue too long, it's also possible to react too quickly to perceived problems. But changing managers too quickly and too frequently is expensive. Every time you fire one manager and hire another, it will cost you money. Your new manager probably won't want to hold the stocks your old manager bought. The new manager's transactions—selling the old positions and buying new ones—will cost you money, perhaps 1 1/2% to 2% or more of the assets allocated to that manager. In addition, there might be legal fees, administrative fees and, very likely, consulting fees.

Summing Up

Part of your job as a fiduciary or trustee is to spot when your money manager is in trouble. Here are some questions to ask:

1. Is there a new portfolio manager on my account?
2. Did any key investment personnel leave?
3. Is the firm a revolving door with rapid, junior-level turn-over?
4. Did the firm lose clients and assets?
5. Is performance slipping?
6. Did the firm's ownership change?
7. Is the firm following the style and approach I hired it to follow?
8. How long am I willing to give the firm to achieve the objectives we agreed upon?
9. Am I correctly interpreting and using performance data to evaluate the success or failure of my manager?
10. Is the firm's investment strategy sound?
11. Could the firm simply be suffering some bad luck?

STEP 8

STEP 8:

Venturing Beyond
Stocks And Bonds

*"Remember the turtle progresses
only when he sticks out his neck."*
ANONYMOUS

O nce investors wander outside the traditional haven of domestic stocks and bonds, they are apt to make a few mistakes. This chapter reviews those mistakes and explains the basics of real estate, international, global and venture capital investments considered to be alternative or nontraditional investments. The use of futures and options and guaranteed investment contracts also is covered.

Mistake #1:   Investors don't consider alternative investments.

The term alternative investments probably was coined because domestic stocks and bonds traditionally have made up the lion's share of institutional and large individual investors' portfolios. Added together, the amount of a typical portfolio invested in guaranteed investment contracts, real estate, international stocks and bonds, venture capital, futures and options and all other alternative investments still is likely to be smaller than the amount invested in either stocks or bonds.

When consultants, money managers and academicians talk about diversification, however, they usually mean more than just stocks and bonds and different manager styles. They're also referring to diversification across several asset classes, and cite statistics to show that this strategy actually can reduce risk and boost returns over the long term.

The graph on page 129 illustrates how diversifying into international equities can increase return while reducing risk. As we discussed in Step 2, the lower the correlation between two classes of assets, the more likely you can improve returns without increasing risk. In this graph, the percentage of the portfolio in international assets increases, yet at 20% international, returns increase at the same time risk decreases.

Mistake #2: They don't allocate enough to alternative investments.

While diversification is thought to reduce risk, it also is supposed to enhance returns. But unless you are willing to make a meaningful commitment to at least one alternative investment class, you won't reap many rewards for your efforts. Most investment professionals suggest a minimum commitment of 5% or, preferably, 10%, to an alternative investment. If you believe diversification will add value, put your money where your mouth is.

Opinions are mixed as to which alternative to invest in first. Many consultants recommend starting with real estate because, as property owners themselves, investors can more easily understand the benefits. Once investors are comfortable with real estate, they say, the next step can be international stocks and/or bonds. Others suggest the opposite, saying international stocks and bonds are a logical investment to complement the domestic stock and bond portfolio. Besides, many corporate executives who double as trustees might work for multinational companies and, therefore, have experience in various countries. Your understanding of how businesses operate in Japan, for example, might give you some insight into the Japanese capital markets.

EFFECT OF DIVERSIFICATION
S&P 500 AND NON-U.S. EQUITY

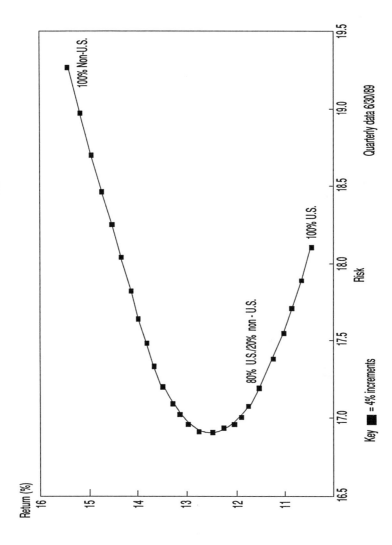

Source: Brinson Partners

Experts abound in all of these investment classes, with consultants and money managers specializing in one or more of them. They'll help you decide whether and how to incorporate real estate, international or another new asset class into your overall asset allocation. But investors must do a lot of homework; otherwise, they will make a third mistake:

Mistake #3:   They don't understand the complexities of the various alternative investment classes.

Here's a brief look at the pros and cons of several of the alternative investments you should be considering for a portion of your assets.

Real Estate

Real estate is best known as an inflation hedge and for its negative correlation with stocks, meaning prices in the real estate market and the domestic stock market historically do not rise and fall in tandem.

Real estate often is the first alternative investment considered by investors. Unlike stocks and bonds, property is a tangible asset. In addition, trustees of Taft-Hartley and some public pension funds prefer real estate over, say, international, because they view real estate as making an investment in jobs and thereby improving economic conditions. Many union and state and municipal funds have real estate programs that favor investing in properties located in the same geographic area in which the participants live and work.

Middle-market investors likely will invest in real estate through commingled funds, where their assets are pooled with money from many other investors, with each owning a piece of several properties to give broad diversification.

Open-end commingled real estate funds have no specific termination dates and accept money continuously. They are more liquid than their closed-end counterparts, but heavy withdrawals from open-end funds can impose hardships on participants who remain. If the sponsor of an open-end fund is hit with a large amount of withdrawal requests, the sponsor might have to sell properties at fire-sale prices to raise the necessary cash, or might have to strip the fund of its best properties because those can be sold the fastest and easiest.

Closed-end funds sell a specific number of units, then close. They have specific termination dates, but participants can't withdraw unless they find other investors to purchase their units.

Some investors, by the way, deliberately purchase other investors' units: That way, they know just what properties they get a percentage of, whereas investors in a new fund are buying into a blind pool without specific properties in it.

You also can make direct purchases of properties. But you'll probably not achieve diversification by geographic location and property type (such as offices, retail and apartments). Just as you don't want to put all of your eggs in a one-investment-class basket, neither do you want to put all of your real estate eggs in a one-property basket.

Mercer Meidinger Hansen, Inc.'s new manager strategy codes divide real estate managers into two camps: One has a narrow focus, investing more than 50% of its assets in a specific property type (such as apartments) or in a specific geographical location (such as the West); the other is broadly diversified, investing in many types of properties and geographical locations, holding retail, office, hotel and industrial properties throughout the United States and without any significant regional bias.

Real estate has two return characteristics. One is income, generated, for example, by rents you collect on an office building or shopping center you own. The other is appreciation, the rise in market value. As the 1980s close, most real estate return has been coming from income, not appreciation.

Investment professionals don't agree on the size at which you should consider investing in real estate. Some suggest waiting until you have $50 million; that way, you can put a sizable chunk into real estate ($5 million, for example) and still have only 10% of your assets in that investment class. Others say you can diversify into real estate at any size, doing so through commingled funds.

International

International securities share many of the pros and cons of domestic stocks and bonds, but offer added risks and rewards because of currency fluctuations and country allocations.

One school of thought suggests you already are investing internationally even if you don't own a Japanese or U.K. stock. If you buy shares of IBM, the theory goes, you're investing internationally because a large chunk of IBM's revenues come from its overseas operations. If you're already doing that, hiring a manager in Japan or London isn't as big a stretch. Still, some union pension funds are reluctant to invest internationally because they fear such investments contribute to the loss of U.S. jobs and economic opportunities.

Some professionals strongly urge investors to hedge currency risk. Much of the good historic performance in international investments has been because of a declining dollar, not just because certain foreign companies are hot.

Here are some of the international manager style categories used by Mercer Meidinger Hansen:

International equity country selection/stock selection managers do an overall review of economic, social and political issues worldwide to make decisions with respect to the allocation of investments between countries and markets other than the client reference country. Then, through fundamental analysis of companies, equities are selected from each of the markets.

International equity stock selection managers identify investments by analyzing through quantitative, technical factors, subjective, judgmental or thematic approaches from markets other than the client reference country. Here, the decision on stock selection overrides decisions on country allocation, currency or other factors.

International equity index managers select and invest in a portfolio of securities to match, to the greatest extent possible, the performance of an index other than for markets within the client reference country. Duplication covers not only returns, but also other characteristics, such as risk, capitalization and country and industry weightings.

International fixed-income/interest active managers make investments in fixed-income securities worldwide, excluding the client's own country. Selection involves both evaluation of currency and values in specific markets. Values are estimated by anticipation of changes in local interest rates. Frequently hedging into the currency of the client reference country is used.

International fixed-income/interest passive managers select investments from outside the client reference country to duplicate the performance of an index, such as the Salomon Brothers Non-U.S. World Government Bond Index.

International balanced managers make investments in equities and fixed-income/interest securities worldwide, excluding those in the client reference country. Issues generally are identified through a top down/bottom up approach applied to each security class.

Endowment funds are relatively aggressive investors in international securities, needing to further diversify away risk. But many also view international as a way to boost returns, which is necessary to make up for any shortfalls in the funds caused by spending principal on various programs.

There are international pooled funds run by banks, insurance companies and mutual funds, all of which make it possible for smaller investors to move into the international arena.

Global

Global investing and international investing are not the same, although some people use the terms interchangeably. U.S. investors making international investments generally exclude either North America or only the United States from their universe of possible countries in which to deploy assets. Those making global investments include North America and the United States.

Global investing is a more recent phenomenon than international, probably due to the growing realization that we all are affected by what happens in our backyard (the United States) next door (Canada) and around the world. When Mercer Meidinger Hansen describes global manager styles in its new manager strategy codes, the same categories are used. The only differences: There is no exclusion of the client's own country, and there are no listings for index or passive managers.

Again, commingled funds are available for global investing as well as for international investing.

Venture Capital

Venture capital generally is thought to be an illiquid investment that takes five to 10 years to mature. The safest way for investors of any size to invest in venture capital is through one or more limited partnerships. That way, your assets are pooled with those of many others and, as in real estate, you own a piece of several deals instead of all of one deal. You could, for example, hire a money manager who will invest your assets in a number of limited partnerships run by several different venture capitalists. Venture capital is a popular investment for endowments and foundations because of its high prospective returns.

One reason those returns can be spectacular, of course, is that the risk of any one deal going sour is high. By investing in more than one partnership, you get added diversification. The kinds of companies the partnerships invest in differ (one may favor the medical field and, another, computers), and wise decisions of the general partner in one partnership will compensate for poor decisions made by another.

Venture capital investments can be made in several stages. Generally, the earlier the stage, the higher the risk and, therefore, the higher the potential return. At the earliest stage, you would be pumping seed money into a firm that has a germ of an idea that needs financing to develop. Or, your money could be used to expand a business or could be pumped in immediately before or after a company goes public.

You likely will be committing your money to venture capitalists: They are the men and women who will seek out the investments and, in all probability, will take an active role in the management and control of the companies in which they invest. Venture capitalists often purchase an equity stake in the company, and become part owners-managers of a sort on behalf of you and the other investors. You are well advised to use a consultant to help screen venture capital partnerships.

GICs

Guaranteed investment contracts (GICs) are insured group annuity contracts issued by major life insurance companies as private placements (that is, deals done outside the mainstream capital markets). Contract terms specify the timing and the amounts of guaranteed interest payments plus return of principal. They also specify contribution dates. Returns usually are above the rates on Treasury securities with the same maturities. Many investors purchase GICs through pooled funds. Be aware, however, that they are difficult to liquidate, and their soundness depends on the financial strength of the insurer from whom you purchase the contract.

Insurers hope to earn a profit by investing the money you place in the GIC in instruments that will, in the aggregate, earn higher returns than they have guaranteed you. They try to achieve that spread by using your money to buy portfolios of real estate and/or high-yield (or junk) bonds and by lending your money to others.

There are several GIC options, including:

- *Bullet GICs.* These are the standard GICs, in which assets are placed with a company in a lump sum at the beginning of the contract, and remain invested for the duration of the contract, which can be up to 20 years. While maturity is fixed, premature withdrawals are limited. The termination value can be book value or market value, whichever is lower.

- *Window GICs.* "Windows" permit periodic deposits during the period of the window, which usually is a year. All deposits receive the guaranteed interest to maturity, generally three to five years. Window GICs are particularly attractive for defined contribution plans such as 401(k) and thrift plans, where participants can direct transfers (at book value) into other, noncompeting investment options.

- *Immediate participation guarantees (IPGs).* IPGs have a minimum guaranteed interest rate that is negotiated annually, and lack a specified maturity. IPGs allow book value withdrawals, but they can create negative cash flow that will affect their yield.

GICs can be purchased directly through an insurance company, possibly through your consultant or with the assistance of a new breed of GIC specialists, who contend they can maximize GIC returns through active management. The idea behind hiring a GIC manager is that he or she spreads out the GICS, with an average maturity of, say, 2 to 2 1/2 years, so they're always turning over. In addition to actively playing interest rates, the GIC manager also watches the credit ratings of the insurance companies issuing the GICs. If the manager shops around and finds that three insurance companies all offer the same rate on a GIC, he'll buy the contract from the firm that has the highest credit rating.

GICs are popular investments for defined contribution plans— where the employees bear the investment risk—because they carry little risk as long as they are held to maturity. They also meet the proposed requirement of the Department of Labor for a guaranteed investment option, in plans such as a 401(k) in which employees are allowed to choose how their assets are to be invested. They are less appropriate for defined benefit plans for, unless the sponsor is very risk averse, higher returns can be achieved elsewhere and at lower cost.

Banks also are beginning to get into the GIC market, offering instruments they call BICs, or bank investment contracts. One way BICs differ from GICs is that the bank contracts offer the same kind of pass-through insurance that investors get on certificates of deposit and other, similar bank investments. There is a move afoot, however, to get Congress to repeal that pass-through insurance.

Futures And Options

Investing in futures and options allows you to hedge your portfolio against price changes that would be unfavorable to the underlying securities you own. Such investments also let you lock in gains and earn some incremental returns.

Farmers have used futures contracts for years to protect themselves against poor prices at harvest time. Indeed, one farmer, a
trustee of a public fund, unknowingly swayed other board members to begin a financial futures program after the fund's investment officer had tried for months to explain futures to the board.
Time and again the board tabled any decision on the investment
because trustees simply didn't understand the concept.

Months later, the fund executive decided to bring up the subject
one more time. On that particular day, a trustee known as Old Ben
was attending his first meeting since spring. When the fund's investment officer mentioned the word "futures," Old Ben reacted
immediately. "I've been using them for years on my corn crop," he
excitedly explained to fellow board members. When the motion
came before the board again that day, it passed. It seems the other
trustees figured if futures made sense to Old Ben, they made sense
to the pension fund.

A futures contract is an agreement to buy or sell, at today's price,
a basket of commodities to be delivered in the future. If you sell a
futures contract, you are contractually bound to hand over the commodities on a given date at today's price, even if the price rises in
the meantime. You have locked in today's price to protect against a
price decline, but you have given up the possibility of profiting
from a future price increase.

When you buy or sell a futures contract, the price is set today,
but the commodity actually will be bought or sold at a future date.
As a buyer, you don't pay the full price for the asset, but rather a
fractional amount (or margin). Although the full price is due upon
delivery to you of the asset, futures contracts rarely are delivered
but, instead, are sold back, or traded, through a futures exchange
before they expire.

Financial futures cover Treasury securities, CDs, GNMA certificates, and other financial instruments. You might buy a financial
futures contract because you expect the underlying instrument to
increase in value by the time it expires. Conversely, you might sell
a financial futures contract because you expect the price to drop.

Options also are contracts. They give the holder the right to buy
or sell an underlying asset at a set price at a set time. There are two
major kinds of options: a put option is the right to sell the underly-

ing asset at a fixed price; a call option is the right to buy that asset at a fixed price.

You can use options to increase income and reduce volatility. If you own a stock and someone pays you $400 for the option to buy that stock, that's $400 you can pocket. If the price of the stock rises, you'll lose the benefit of the increased price of the stock because the other party will exercise his or her option to buy your stock at the agreed-upon, lower price. But you'll still have the $400. If the stock price dips, the $400 will help cushion your loss. You'll likely still own the stock, however, because the other party won't want to exercise the option to buy the stock at the agreed-upon price, which was higher than its current market price.

Some money managers will hedge your portfolio through the use of futures, or will write options on your portfolio, if you give them permission.

Summing Up

Investing in real estate, international, venture capital, futures and options and other alternatives to stocks and bonds can help you achieve diversification, that is, increase return and decrease risk.

Before you decide whether or not to add alternative investments to your portfolio, ask yourself:

1. How much am I willing to commit to alternative invest-ments? Am I willing to allocate enough (5% to 10% per asset class) to make a difference in achieving my risk and return objectives?

2. Do I understand how investments in real estate, internation-al, global, venture capital and futures and options work?

3. Do I have a professional (such as a consultant) who is well-versed in the alternative asset class I have chosen, who will do the research and due diligence it will take to find the right money managers and investment vehicles?

STEP 9

STEP 9:

Hiring An Investment Management Consultant

"Beware the articulate incompetent."
ANONYMOUS

Whether you need all the help you can get, or whether you'd really rather do everything yourself, you should understand what an investment management consultant can do for you.

If you hire the right one, your consultant can provide value-added services that, in the long run, will have a significant impact on the investment results of your fund. A consultant can help you:

- Establish an investment policy statement and choose an asset allocation plan that follows that policy.

- Decide what money management styles you should be seeking.

- Evaluate and select money managers.

- Monitor the performance of your fund and your managers.

- Diversify your portfolio beyond traditional stocks and bonds.

In the process, your consultant can serve as your teacher, especially if investing isn't your full-time job. And because investors and money managers don't seem to speak the same language, your consultant can be your interpreter. This chapter explains the services consultants provide, and will show you how to evaluate and select the consultant who, in turn, will help you oversee the investment management of your portfolio.

The investment management consulting industry, which emerged in the 1960s around the issue of performance measurement, since has grown beyond merely providing performance data. In fact, you might not even need help with performance evaluation, so the first decision you need to make is what you want your consultant to do for you. For example, you might only want help with selecting a new money manager. Or, you might want the consultant to assist you with everything covered in this book, plus trustee arrangements, plan administration and custodial services.

Ideally, consultants would like you to hire them to create from scratch, or to finely tune and improve, your total investment program. They'd like to work with you from the beginning (setting risk/return objectives) to the end (monitoring your fund). In reality, however, consultants often are hired only for the final steps—hiring managers and evaluating performance. Once these tasks have been completed and the investor has developed confidence in the consultant, then the consultant is more likely to be asked to help with strategic issues, such as asset allocation. In other cases, a trustee's first dealings with a consultant could be on the actuarial and/or benefits side. Many firms specializing in actuarial consulting now offer broader investment management consulting services too; they can take you from the point that you first set up a plan through the performance measurement step. Many middle-market investors probably use a consultant for the first time to help set goals and objectives and write a policy statement.

As is the case with many decisions you'll make about your investment program, there is no consensus about the best time to call in a consultant.

Some investors, previously concerned solely with preservation of capital, seek outside assistance when they recognize the need to increase returns or diversify their portfolios. Your decision likely will be more qualitative than quantitative. As your assets increase, you might become uncomfortable with the investment responsibility. Or perhaps you find yourself spending so much time talking to participants that there's little time left to oversee investments. Most likely, you simply feel you don't have the time and energy to become an investment expert in addition to being an expert at your profession. If you are at all uncertain that the assets you're responsible for are being prudently invested, that's a clue you should at least talk to a consultant.

Before you jump into the water, though, familiarize yourself with the mistakes others have made in dealing with consultants.

Mistake #1: "I don't need a consultant; I can hire money managers."

Anyone can hire a money manager. With thousands to choose from, you could simply throw a dart at a list and choose your manager that way. But a consultant can help you hire the right manager by screening a list of candidates to your risk and return objectives, your asset allocation choices and your more subjective criteria.

If trustees "can sit through an entire meeting and know exactly what the manager is saying, then maybe they don't need a consultant," says consultant Jack Marco. Otherwise, he says, the trustees can use their consultant to translate the jargon into English and to make sure the manager gives the client the information he needs. A good consultant knows the managers, has researched them thoroughly, and views them with a healthy dose of skepticism that will serve you well. "Even if you understand everything the manager says, you might not know it's bull; that's where a consultant can help," asserts Ronald Surz, principal of Becker, Burke Associates, Inc.

Besides, assisting with manager searches is just a small part of what an investment management consulting firm does. Most consultants view the hiring of money managers as only one of many steps in structuring the investment process and enhancing performance. Some consultants are reluctant to accept manager search assignments if that's the only task they're given. That's because they believe even the best manager ultimately could fail unless your investment structure is properly established and monitored.

Consultants also can help trustees focus their time on the right areas. Your consultant will point out, for example, that if you spend 90% of your time overseeing equity managers, even though 60% of your assets are in bonds, you either should direct more of your attention to the fixed-income area, or consider changing direction. Consultants also can help investors overcome the fear of the unknown about other asset classes.

Mistake #2:   "Consultants demand too much of my time."

True, your investment management consultant might ask you to fill out a questionnaire that could take an hour or more to complete. Then the consultant will want to discuss your answers. And all of that time will be spent before he or she actually sits down to work with you on your investments.

From the questionnaire, the consultant will learn your expectations of the fund and your level of sophistication about the financial markets, enabling him/her to be on the same wavelength with you in relation to performance, risk, market cycles, etc.

Investing time at the beginning of the process can save you enormous amounts of time later on. Being a fund trustee isn't a full-time job, so you aren't expected to know how to measure risk, set realistic rate of return objectives and choose among asset classes. If you attempt this task yourself, it very well could become a full-time job. Such matters are a consultant's domain; even though the process seems lengthy, your consultant has data at his/her fingertips and a level of expertise that would take you months or even years to develop on your own.

Mistake #3:   "I don't need a consultant; I'll let my manager perform all those tasks."

An important rule to remember: The money managers manage your money; you manage the money managers.

You need to set realistic guidelines within which the manager will operate. *You*, not the manager, must control these guidelines.

Mistake #4: "Then I'll just let the consultant make all of the decisions."

Consultants are there to advise you. It's their job to help you do your job better, not to do your job for you. You have—and must retain—control over your assets. If your plan is covered by ERISA, you, not the consultant, will be held accountable under the law to the plan participants. Besides, consultants don't have all the answers. Instead, they make it their job to know the right questions to ask. They'll keep you abreast of industry trends, new developments and, in effect, will be your window to the world of investment management.

Also, consultants need monitoring just as managers do. You should set and implement performance guidelines for your consultant: Has your investment strategy paid off? Are your goals more specific and realistic? Did your consultant help reduce investment management, custodial and other fees? Did your consultant invite you to seminars and educational forums? Was your manager selection process enhanced? Did your consultant set up a system of checks and balances you and your managers can follow?

"Consultants should be able to document the results of their advice, such as how their asset allocation recommendations fared compared to the market over time and the performance of (their) clients versus the risk they were exposed to," says consultant John A. Vann, senior vice president for performance evaluation services at Dean Witter Reynolds, Inc.

Vann also warns that investors might wind up serving as referees between managers and the consultant. When you introduce a new consultant to your old money manager, be prepared for fireworks. The manager could be worried about getting fired if he or she isn't prominent in the consultant's stable of money managers. And, yes, many consultants have favorite managers within their universes. They're human, and they have biases, particularly in money manager selection. If you use a consultant to assist in hiring new managers, make sure the consultant allows your existing managers to be included in the competition.

Mistake #5:   "I don't need a consultant once I've set policy, made asset allocation decisions and hired managers."

You don't simply hire managers and walk away. As we discussed in Step 6, once you know where you're going, you need to determine if you're staying on target and, if you're not, how to get back on course.

Your consultant will assist you in monitoring the performance of your managers, periodically reevaluating your goals and objectives and reexamining your asset allocation as market conditions change. Your consultant will also perform such specific tasks as determining whether the same people and investment process are in place at the firms you hired.

Mistake #6:   "Consultants are a needless expense."

With their expertise on investment policy, asset allocation and hiring and monitoring managers, consultants can help you maximize the performance of your portfolio. In some cases, they also can help you turn your fund into a profit center. If your fund can earn an additional $1 million in investment income, which would reduce the amount your company contributes to the plan, it seems worthwhile to spend $30,000 on a consultant. Remember, a one percentage point increase in investment return can, over time, cut your annual contribution by 15% to 20%.

One national consultant says that six years ago, he began to track the performance of managers hired on his recommendation. When he compared their returns to those of all the managers in his universe, those hired by his clients were in the top 10%. That is value added!

Mistake #7:   "I'll definitely hire one of the big, national firms."

You don't have to hire a huge consulting operation to get quality services. Indeed, some investors favor smaller shops. They believe if they hire a big firm, they might get lost among the billion-dollar clients. By all means, check out the household names in the industry, but don't overlook regional firms and broker consultants that have documented results and references you can check.

Mistake #8: "I can get consulting services for free."

There's no such thing as a free lunch, whether it's in relation to your main line of business or to your investments. In theory, you can obtain investment management consulting services without ever writing a check, but you're still paying for the services indirectly.

Many consultants accept soft-dollar payments for their services. That means they are compensated by the trades done in your portfolio. The question is: Are you getting good execution of your trades, or are your soft-dollar payments costing you real money in net return because of sloppy trading?

The process isn't always as simple as it sounds, though. If your fund largely is passively managed (such as an index fund), the fund might not generate sufficient trades to pay the consultant's fee.

Conversely, you might generate far more trades than are needed to pay the consultant's fee. What happens to those commission dollars? Make sure there is a process by which your consultant notifies you of the progress made toward payment of his/her fee and that your contract with the consultant specifies what happens to the excess commission dollars.

There's no question that a consultant paid with soft dollars can substantially increase his/her income by high turnover of securities in your portfolio. Check your statements carefully, and make sure you're comfortable with the amount of buying and selling being done in your portfolio, and that it is consistent with your investment policy.

The alternative to purchasing consulting services through soft-dollar arrangements is the direct payment to the consultant in hard dollars. Hard-dollar fees vary from hourly rates of $100 to $200 to tens of thousands of dollars in retainer fees for larger plans.

Mistake #9:   Not considering wrap fees.

"Wrap fees were specifically developed to address the potential conflict of interest between the broker consultant and his clients," says Len Reinhart, senior vice president, independent advisory programs/consulting services department, of Shearson Lehman Hutton. "I believe the wrap fee is a genuine win-win-win situation for all concerned—the client, the consultant and the money manager."

Critics, however, contend investors could wind up paying more under wrap fees than they would if they purchased the services separately. They also say that clients with wrap fees must do all their trades with one brokerage firm, which could reduce the chances of getting the best execution.

The difference between wrap fees and traditional investment management-related fees can be compared to the difference between health maintenance organizations (HMOs) and traditional medical insurance:

HMO participants pay high premiums, and, in return, all medical-related treatment is free, no matter how frequently the patient needs medical attention. With traditional insurance, premiums are much lower, but the patient usually has to pay a deductible plus a percentage of most medical-related treatment costs, with total medical costs dependent on how often the patient requires medical assistance.

Wrap fees may seem high (typically 1 1/2% to 3% annually of your assets), but they cover several investment-related services, including: help in setting goals and objectives and writing the investment policy statement; help in selecting money managers and monitoring performance. Wrap fees also include all transaction costs, custodial services as well as the manager's own fees. Under the more traditional fee structure, investors pay for each service separately, with total costs dependent on how many services are required and what fee schedules are negotiated.

Investors who use wrap fees say they'd rather know up front how much they'll pay in fees, rather than risk surprises later. Wrap fees most often are offered by consultants who work for brokerage firms or have clearing relationships with them. Most consultants base their wrap fee on managers' normal portfolio turnover, the services the client likely will need and the normal brokerage discount the client would get.

Wrap fees are more common today for retail accounts than for institutional portfolios. However, some broker-consultants believe wrap fees have a place in institutional portfolios.

"Five years from now, I predict wrap fees will be the norm for many middle-market accounts," contends Dennis R. White, senior vice president, consulting services department, Shearson Lehman Hutton.

Mistake #10: Not realizing your consultant may have conflicts of interest.

Learn what motivates your consultant from a profit standpoint and be alert to any potential conflicts of interest. One potential conflict arises if the consultant doesn't disclose whether his/her firm also receives compensation from investment managers. For example, some consultants sell managers data they collect from funds and other sources, the same way they sell, to you, data collected from managers. Ideally, says consultant Jack Marco, a consulting firm should earn 100% of its income from services provided to plan sponsors. If the firm does provide services to money managers for a fee, that, too, should be disclosed. "Always ask the consultant, 'Who else is paying you?' to determine how objective the consultant is," Marco advises.

It's unusual, but possible, for the consultant to collect a finder's fee from a manager each time he/she makes a match between an investor and that manager. "That's an incentive for the consultant to have you fire and hire managers," sometimes unnecessarily, warns Howard Pohl, principal of Becker, Burke Associates.

Another troubling possibility is for a consultant to charge a money manager to be included in the universe of managers he presents to his clients. Pohl says some consultants require managers who want to be included in their universe to subscribe to some service or to direct all brokerage through the consultant if a client

hires that manager. Find out where the consultant you're considering stands on this and other issues we've discussed in this step.

Mistake #11: "All consultants are alike."

Like money managers, consultants come in all shapes, forms and
sizes. Some are independent, some are affiliated with a national actuarial or brokerage firm. Their experience level runs the gamut
from highly sophisticated and seasoned to the out-and-out
neophyte. The good ones, though, share some common characteristics: personal integrity, professional competence, maturity in investment judgment, a strong sense of third-party objectivity and
genuine interest and concern in the long-term well-being of their
clients.

Mistake #12: "I don't care about the consultant's relationship with money managers."

Don't underestimate the relationship between the consultant and
the manager. Money manager Ken Fisher says investors should ask
consultants how much money they have placed with the firms they
are recommending. If most of a manager's assets came from one
consultant, chances are that consultant "owns the manager," Fisher
warns. It's also possible for the manager to "own" the consultant.
Either way, you aren't getting the objective advice you're paying
for.

In theory, every manager should have a chance to be hired in
every search; you must determine if that happens in reality. A consultant who keeps bringing the same manager together with most
of his/her clients either doesn't have a genuinely large universe of
managers or is turning the manager selection process into a self-ful-
filling prophecy.

But overestimating the consultant's relationship can be just as
dangerous. Fisher suggests asking the consultant, "Have you visited
the manager in his shop?" Investors assume, sometimes incorrectly,
that the consultant has made these due diligence calls, yet he and

others tell of consultants whose manager universe is created with borrowed information, and isn't based on personal, first-hand experience and knowledge.

If you're looking for someone to help you find the hottest-performing managers, Fisher also has another pointed question to ask: "Give me a list of managers with $1 billion to $2 billion (under management) who have emerged over the last couple of years. How many did you identify before they had $500 million?" Then, ask for documentation. According to Fisher's theory, broker consultants often fare better in this area than many institutional consulting firms. That's because some big consulting operations won't recommend a money management firm until it has grown to at least $1 billion under management, he says, causing them to miss the opportunity of discovering leading-edge managers. On the other hand, certain institutional consulting firms (including Rogers, Casey & Associates and Collins and Associates) specialize in identifying embryonic-stage managers.

Mistake #13: "I'll simply hire one of the consultants who has called on me."

The search for the right consultant should be as systematic as the search for the right money manager. It's not a hit-or-miss proposition.

Dale Stevens, partner with Wilshire Associates, spends most his working hours dealing with the independent consultants who are part of the Wilshire Cooperative. He provides these hints to investors:

"One of the most important things is to feel very comfortable with the consultant as confidant, just as you would with outside (legal) counsel your firm would hire." The consultant, the company's chief executives and the trustees must have "a good fit in terms of the philosophical approach to managing the plan," says Stevens. For example, they all must be on the same wavelength regarding whether they consider the employee benefit plan to be a profit center or a liability.

Stevens divides consultants into three camps: those who are academically trained, and specialize in technology and the capital markets; those who are generalists, and function as overall financial consultants; and those who combine aspects of the other two.

Stevens believes the consultant also must function as an "advocate of the plan sponsor's philosophy." And the consultant should be comfortable with the region of the country in which the client is located. Stevens says the consultant should understand the regional economy, the special needs of the beneficiaries and any peculiarities of doing business in that part of the country.

Among the questions Stevens advises you to ask before hiring a consultant:

- What are your technological capabilities?

- What is the basis of your knowledge of the investment community, and, particularly, of money managers?

- What due diligence do you perform on the managers you actively follow and recommend to clients?

- How timely does your firm provide performance reports following the close of each quarter?

- How often would you meet with me?

- Who would be meeting with me? (Is it the same person who initially called on you? Sometimes, a senior-level staffer is around until the firm is hired, but then disappears and leaves the ongoing servicing to a subordinate.) If I see a junior staffer, will he or she be able to speak to the issues or is he/she essentially a messenger who simply delivers a measurement product?

You should investigate the consultants' professional training, years in the financial industry, client references and examples of performance reports and other work they have done. Are the reports tailored to a client's specific needs or are they "off the shelf"?

To determine which consultants to interview for the job, says Charles Thomas, co-publisher of *Consultant Compendium*, get information on the size of the staff, number of key professionals, a client list (which gives clues about the size and type of clients) and services offered. Much of that information is available from Thomas' profiles, from the consultants' directory issue published each fall by *Pensions & Investments,* and from the *Money Market Directory.*

Thomas knows a consultant who complained that he and his peers are being subjected to the same sort of close scrutiny to which consultants subject investment managers. The consultant wasn't thrilled at the prospect of filling out lengthy questionnaires and making competitive presentations. Thomas, on the other hand, is delighted. "It's high time consultants got a bit of their own medicine," he says.

Summing Up

An investment management consultant can help you put all of the pieces of the investment puzzle together. You can hire a consultant to work with you from the point you begin to set risk and return objectives, or you can hire a consultant only to help you hire money managers or to monitor the performance of your fund. The consultant will help you manage your money managers, but you must manage the consultant.

The process of hiring a consultant is similar to the process of hiring an investment manager. In beginning the search, consider taking these steps suggested by F. Jerome Grimm, co-publisher of *Consultant Compendium:*

1. Did I write a position statement on my fund and the sponsoring organization and send it to each candidate?
2. Did I prepare specifications for the proposed consulting assignment?
3. Did I construct a questionnaire for the candidates?
4. Did I send the statement, specifications and questionnaire to each candidate, asking them to call if they're not interested in the assignment and to fill out the questionnaire promptly if they are interested? (Give the candidates 30 days to

respond, then begin the evaluation when the cutoff date passes.)

5. Did I use a matrix to tabulate responses and identify finalists I will interview?

6. Did I give ample time (approximately an hour) for the interviews? Did I leave at least a half-hour between interviews to discuss the candidate while his/her presentations are still fresh in my mind?

7. Once I hire a consultant, will I have an initial meeting? Things to be discussed include: specific tasks, a timetable to get them done, communication channels and a meeting schedule.

STEP 10

STEP 10:

Surviving
"Investment-Speak"

*"An economist is an expert who will know tomorrow why the
things he predicted yesterday didn't happen today."*
LAURENCE J. PETER

This final step is dedicated to every board member, trustee or
individual investor who has ever sat through—and endured—
an investment meeting obfuscated by jargon.

All professionals, of course, love jargon. It makes them feel elite;
it keeps nosy outsiders from knowing more than they should; it
furthers the mystique surrounding what they do; and perhaps most
importantly, it provides a wonderful smoke screen for fuzzy thinking.

And for investment professionals, jargon can also serve as a useful marketing tool; there's probably not a money manager or consultant alive who has not at least once thought to himself, "If I can't
dazzle them with brilliance, I'll bafffle them with B.S."

That is why we have put together this glossary of "Investment-
Speak." A better understanding of the lingo of the trade should
both help you better evaluate a prospective manager and communi-
cate with the one you hire. And, we hope, it will also serve as a
survival kit for money manager meetings.

Accommodative Monetary Policy: The Federal Reserve policy of increasing the supply of money to make credit more readily available. An "easy money" policy tends to lower interest rates, particularly short-term rates, and is therefore generally bullish for stocks and bonds. In contrast, a *restrictive monetary policy*, which results in "tight money," generally has a negative near-term effect on securities prices.

Actual(s): Refers to the physical commodity as compared with a futures contract on that commodity.

ADR (American Depository Receipts): An easy way to lose money on foreign stocks without ever leaving home. Certificates of ownership of a foreign-based corporation that are being held by U.S. banks. Instead of buying shares of a foreign corporation in foreign markets, Americans can buy shares in the U.S. in the form of an ADR, thus eliminating the need to convert currencies or to transfer certificates internationally.

Air Pocket: When a stock drops rapidly and without warning, it is said to have hit an "air pocket."

Alligator Spread: An option spread so "convoluted" that the investor runs the risk of being "eaten alive" by commissions.

Alpha T-Statistic, Beta Coefficient, R-Squared: Terms frequently used by investment management consultants to impress/intimidate clients and prospects.

Arbitrage: The simultaneous purchase and sale of the same or an equivalent security in order to profit from price differentials. For example, if IBM trades at $100 on the New York Stock Exchange (NYSE) and at $99-1/2 on the Midwest Stock Exchange (MSE), an investor could guarantee a profit by selling IBM on the NYSE and buying IBM on the MSE, provided that the difference was sufficient to cover trading costs.

Asset Redeployment: The reallocation of a firm's underutilized assets in order to improve efficiency and profitability.

Asset Value: A measure of a corporation's overall worth based on the total amount of net assets, as opposed to valuation methods which analyze earnings and dividends. For example, a paper company may operate inefficiently and earn minimal profits, but hold extensive assets such as timber and real estate, thereby making the stock far more valuable on an asset basis than on its public market valuation. Frequently such securities, because they lack the visibility of earnings or because there are no expectations of the timely realization of the underlying asset values, will trade at steep discounts to asset value. Such securities are often referred to as *asset plays* and are considered strong candidates for takeovers.

At the Margin: A favorite term of business school graduates, which is difficult to define precisely, but generally refers to incremental or marginal change.

Averaging Down: An investment technique of purchasing the same security at successively lower prices in order to reduce the average cost of a share of stock. *Averaging up* calls for purchase of the same security at successively higher prices, in order to accumulate a stock while maintaining an average cost that is lower than the current market price.

Baby Bond: A bond with a face value of less than $1,000.

Backwardation: An unusual situation in the commodities market when the cash (spot) price is higher than the futures (forward) price. Usually the reverse is true because of the "cost-of-carry" (see Contango).

Basis Point (BP): 100 basis points equal one percentage point. For example, there is a 20 basis point difference between two bonds if one yields 8.4% and the other yields 8.6%.

Bear: Someone who believes stock or bond prices will decline.

Bearding: Instead of placing one large order through a single broker (thereby tipping his hand), a portfolio manager might break the order into smaller pieces. This practice is referred to as "bearding."

Bear Trap: A "head fake" on the downside.

Bed & Breakfast: Traders' jargon for the sale of a security near the close of the market and the repurchase of the same security the following morning.

Beige Book: A summary of economic conditions in each of the twelve federal reserve bank districts compiled before every Federal Open Market Committee Meeting. To "Fed watchers," the beige book provides important clues as to the likely direction of monetary policy.

Belgian Dentist: Europe's equivalent of an "odd lotter."

Big Four: The four major Japanese brokerage firms—Daiwa, Nikko, Nomura, & Yamaichi.

Binomial Random Variable, Curvilinear Correlation, & Multicollinearity: Statistical terms to throw back at your consultant to intimidate him or her!

Black Box: In money management jargon, a term referring to a proprietary approach to investment decision-making that is both quantitative and mysterious, and which is characterized by its practitioner's reluctance to fully explain the methodology. The ultimate "trust me" approach to managing money.

Black Monday: October 19, 1987, when the Dow Jones Industrial Average fell 508 points, or 22.6 percent. To this day the New York Stock Exchange officially maintains the setback was not a crash (that dreaded "C" word) but only "a major technical correction."

Black-Scholes Option Pricing Model: A mathematical formula that calculates the value of an option based on the price of the underlying stock, the strike price, the period until the option expires, the stock's price volatility, and the current risk-free interest rate. If this sounds like jargon try deciphering the *binomial option pricing model*.

Blip: Refers to a minor fluctuation in the market, either up or down.

Blow It Out: When a trader is instructed to sell a stock immediately, at any price.

"Blow Off": The final, usually climactic phase of a strong market advance.

Bottom Fishing: A strategy of attempting to purchase stocks at the very bottom of their trading ranges. In extreme cases, bottom fishers buy securities of bankrupt or near bankrupt firms.

Bourse: French word (meaning purse) commonly used to describe the Paris Stock Exchange. Also refers to the exchanges in Switzerland and Belgium.

Breadth of Market: Refers to the number of advancing versus declining issues and is an indicator of the underlying strength of a market movement.

Breakup Value: The overall value of the individual pieces of a company if sold separately. Although most stocks will trade at discounts to their breakup value, significant discrepancies between market value and breakup value often indicate inefficient operations and management, thereby attracting the interest of corporate raiders.

Bull: Someone who believes stock and bond prices will rise.

Bull Trap: A "head fake" on the upside.

Bunds: German Treasuries.

Busted Convertible: A convertible whose "conversion price" (the price at which a convertible security can be converted into common stock) is significantly higher than the price of the underlying stock. Thus, the "conversion privilege" has no value.

Buying/Selling Climax: A sudden, climactic end to a trend, characterized by high volatility and extremely high volume.

Callable: A bond that can be redeemed by the issuer before maturity. Most bonds offer some "call protection" to the investor. Many high-coupon bonds are vulnerable to being called in periods of declining interest rates.

Called Away: Term used when a callable bond has, in fact, been called; also used when the writer of a call option has the underlying stock "called away."

Capital Flight: The transfer of funds out of a country to avoid risks such as currency depreciation or the confiscation of assets during periods of political or economic instability.

Capital Goods: Goods such as machinery and heavy equipment used in the production of other goods.

Capital Markets: The various markets in which long-term debt and equity securities are bought and sold.

Cash Cow: A business that generates a high cash flow.

Cash Equivalents: Securities such as Treasury bills or money market funds that can be readily converted into cash.

Cash Flow Analysis: An increasingly popular method of security analysis that focuses on "cash streams" as opposed to reported earnings (which can often be highly distorted due to extraordinary items and accounting gimmickry). *Free* or *undedicated cash flow* can be used to increase dividends, buy back company shares or reduce debt, thereby enhancing shareholder value.

"Catalysts": Wall Street euphemism for corporate raiders.

Cats and Dogs: Slang for speculative securities. "Emerging" dogs are referred to as "puppies."

Cats, Tigers, Lions: Acronyms for "stripped" Treasury bonds.

Central Bank: The institution responsible for a country's monetary policy. In the U.S. the central bank is called the Federal Reserve (or Fed); in the U.K. it is referred to as The Bank of England; West Germany's central bank is called the Bundesbank; in Japan it is known as the Bank of Japan.

Chartist: Someone who believes that the future trend of stock prices can be divined by studying wiggles & squiggles on a sheet of graph paper. Such a person is also likely to believe in Santa Claus and the Tooth Fairy.

"Circuit Breakers" and "Side Cars": Nicknames for program trading restrictions put on by the NYSE and the Chicago Merc to prevent the stock market from falling too far too fast.

Closet Indexing: Refers to an "active" investment manager who seeks to avoid underperforming the market by constructing a portfolio that simply mirrors the broad market averages.

Collateralized Bond Obligation (CBO): A sure winner of the what-will-Wall Street-think-up-next contest. A CBO is a "package" of junk bond financings that banks, insurance companies and others try to palm off on other institutional investors in an attempt to lower their exposure to the crumbling world of junk. A CBO is similar in principle to the children's game, "hot potato."

Combination Write: The sale of call and put options on a stock already owned. Also referred to as a "covered strangle sale."

Commodity Research Bureau Index: The CRB's index of twenty-seven commodity futures prices.

Confirmation: When two or more technical indicators are pointing in the same direction (up or down), thus "confirming" each other.

Consolidation: Differs from a "correction" in that the decline is usually limited to 10 percent.

Constant Dollars: Inflation-adjusted dollars that provide a more accurate gauge of true purchasing power than do nominal dollars.

Constructive: Less than bullish but not bearish.

Contango: The normal condition in the commodities market when the futures (forward) price is higher than the cash (spot) price.

Converts: Slang for convertible bonds.

Convexity: A measure of the sensitivity of a bond's price to changing interest rates. It's enough to make you want to stay away from bonds!

Core Holdings: "Put away" stocks.

Correction: A sharp reaction or fall in the price of a security or market index after a sustained price increase. Technical analysts often perceive this as beneficial because markets don't move up in a straight line: i.e. "trees don't grow to the sky" (whatever that means).

Covered Call Writing: A conservative options strategy that involves purchasing securities and simultaneously writing (selling) call options on them. A covered call writer receives the dividends from the underlying security as well as the premium income from the call option. Also referred to as a *buy and write strategy*.

CPI (Consumer Price Index): A monthly measure of the relative cost of living compared with a base year (currently 1967), which is constructed by U.S. Bureau of Labor statistics according to the spending patterns of an urban family of four.

Crown Jewel: The "prized catch" of a company. Also referred to as "raider bait."

Current Account Balance: The value of all exports of goods and services less all imports (merchandise trade balance), plus net receipts of interest, profits, and dividends from abroad. The broadest measure of trade, the current account may be either a surplus or a deficit. Also known as the *balance-of-payments*.

Cutting A Melon: When a company declares an unusually large dividend.

Cyclical Stocks: Stocks of companies whose profits tend to be heavily influenced by cyclical changes in general economic activity, such as steels, chemicals and papers, that often reach their tops and bottoms well before the general economy.

Data Paralysis: A "trap" that anyone managing money can easily fall into—the hesitation or unwillingness to "move" or take action on an investment decision until one more "confirming" piece of data comes in.

Dead-Cat Bounce: A free-falling stock will usually "rebound" once it hits bottom, even though it has no "life" left in it.

Dead Money: A "sleeper" stock that never wakes up.

Dedication: A form of "passive" fixed-income management in which a bond portfolio is structured so its cash flow matches a defined stream of liability payments.

Defensive Stocks: Stocks, such as electric utilities, foods, tobaccos and drugs, that are relatively immune to the vicissitudes of business cycles and thus tend to resist general market declines.

Deflation: What happens after a money manager has carefully constructed a portfolio to cope with inflation.

Delta: A favorite buzzword of the options crowd. The theoretical change in the price of an option given a one-point change in the price of the underlier (I think).

Derivatives: Securities, such as futures, options, or swaps, that derive their value from another security. Such securities are said to trade in the "shadow market."

Dirt Bonds: Securities issued by the Farmers' Home Administration.

Discount Bond: A bond that currently sells at a price that is less than its par value (because its coupon is below going market rates), thus affording investors the opportunity of capital gains if held until maturity. A *deep discount bond* sells at a substantial discount from par value (often 20 percent or more). Such bonds are highly volatile and will appreciate rapidly as interest rates fall and drop precipitously as rates rise.

Discounted: "Taken into account"; standard line given by Wall Street "experts" to explain why a stock didn't react to an announcement that was widely expected to move its price sharply. Example—"the market had already discounted the drop in the prime rate."

Discount Rate: The interest rate charged by the Federal Reserve on loans to its member banks. Along with open market operations and reserve requirements, a major tool by which the Fed implements its monetary policy.

Disinflationary Stocks: Stocks that tend to benefit from a slowing in the rate of inflation, including such high-yielding stocks as electric utilities and telephones.

Divergence: Occurs when one technical indicator points in one direction and another indicator points in another direction.

Dividend Capture: A trading strategy (practiced mainly by Japanese corporations because of favorable tax treatment) that entails the purchase of a stock just prior to its going "ex dividend," thus becoming the holder-of-record, then selling it immediately afterward to "capture" the dividend.

Dividend Discount Model: An important equity valuation model used by investment professionals to determine the price at which a security should sell based on the discounted or *present value* of expected dividend payments.

DM: Deutsche (German) marks.

DOL: Acronym for the Department of Labor, which administers and enforces the Employee Retirement Income Security Act of 1974. ERISA sets standards for the fiduciary conduct of trustees, investment managers, and other parties responsible for overseeing and investing private pension fund assets.

Don't Fight the Tape: A commonly used investment term meaning an investor should not trade against the market trend ("Let the trend be your friend"). While not grounded in academic theory, this slogan is frequently good advice.

Downside/Downside Risk: The potential loss that may be incurred by making an investment. A stock is said to have limited downside risk (or downside protection) if it is selling near the bottom of its historic trading range or has significant earnings, dividends or asset value to support its price at its current level.

Downtick: A drop in the price of a security from its previous price; the opposite of an *uptick.*

Drop Lock: A floating-rate note that automatically converts to a fixed-rate note if interest rates drop to a specified level.

Dumbbell: What the market makes everyone look like from time to time. A strategy of concentrating bond holdings in very short and very long maturities.

Durable Goods: Products that have a prolonged useful life (children's toys need not apply), including autos, appliances, and furniture (consumer durables) as well as machinery and equipment (producer durables).

Duration: Fixed-income managers love this one! In simple terms, duration is a measure of the price sensitivity of a bond or bond portfolio given a change in interest rates. *Stochastic duration*—any money manager caught using this term in a client service meeting should be fired for "poor communication!"

Earnings Predictability: Wall Street prizes companies with high earnings "visibility"—earnings that grow at a sustained, above-average rate—and almost always rewards such companies with a "premium multiple." On the other hand, nothing roils money managers more than "negative earnings surprises"—reported earnings that fall short of management's rosy forecasts or analyst's expectations.

Economic Indicators: *Leading indicators,* such as money supply growth, corporate profits, and stock prices, generally reach peaks or troughs before the corresponding points are reached in overall economic activity. *Coincident indicators,* including retail sales, industrial production, and the number of employees on nonagricultural payrolls, generally reach peaks or troughs at approximately the same time as the aggregate business cycle. *Lagging indicators,* such as the prime rate and the unit cost of labor, generally reach peaks or troughs after the corresponding points are reached in overall economic activity.

ECU: European currency unit; a basket of *common market currencies.*

Efficient Market: A securities market in which prices accurately reflect all available knowledge and adjust immediately to any new information. Academicians who subscribe to the *Efficient Market Hypothesis* maintain that a professional money manager can only achieve consistently superior investment results by taking greater than market risk.

Efficient Portfolio: A securities portfolio (based on modern portfolio theory) that offers the maximum expected return for any given level of risk, or the minimum amount of risk for any expected return.

Elbow: The maturity on the yield curve where you get the most bang for your buck.

Enhanced Indexing: Not content to merely being "average," index-fund managers increasingly are developing "active" investment strategies within a passive framework with the expectation of outperforming (and not just matching) a target benchmark (such as the S&P 500). This can be done by "tilting" the indexed portfolio toward favored market sectors.

Eurodollar Bond: A dollar-denominated bond sold to investors outside the U.S. that pays interest and principal in Eurodollars. This method of financing can be attractive to U.S. corporations, because there are fewer regulatory delays and costs involved in the Euromarket, and because they can sometimes be sold at lower interest rates than in the U.S.

Eurodollars: Short-term, dollar-denominated bank deposits held outside the U.S. Eurodollars are generally used to settle international transactions, although investors often transfer funds overseas to benefit from higher interest rates.

Europe 1992: The target date for eliminating trade barriers between the twelve member nations of the European Economic Community, thus creating the world's largest market and trading bloc.

Event Risk: The risk to bondholders that a merger, restructuring, or other unpredictable outside event may negatively impact the price of that corporation's securities.

Excess Return: Refers either to the difference between the return on a security or portfolio in excess of the return available on a risk-free asset (T-Bills), or the return in excess of a market index (S&P 500) given a comparable level of risk (*alpha*).

Exposure: Risk.

Fallen Angel: A once high-flying "growth stock" that has since come crashing down to earth.

Fed Funds Rate: The interest rate member banks charge each other for overnight loans needed to meet reserve requirements; considered a sensitive indicator of the Fed's monetary policy since it is set daily by market forces.

Fibonacci Retracement: Following a strong price move, some market technicians believe that a stock is apt to "retrace" or "give up" either 38.2% or 61.8% of the move, percentages derived from the Fibonacci sequence.

Figuring the Tail: Corporate finance jargon; it refers to pricing a competitive underwriting bid, literally down to the last decimal point.

Financial Futures: Futures contracts on Treasury bills, notes, bonds, CDs, GNMA certificates or foreign currencies.

First-In, First-Out (FIFO): A method of inventory valuation that also explains how insiders make money in the stock market.

Five Percent Rule: Law requiring anyone purchasing five percent or more of a public company's stock to disclose their holdings and their intentions. A *toehold purchase* is the accumulation of just under five percent of the outstanding shares.

Flash GNP: Preliminary estimate of the economy's growth in the most recent quarter. Wall Streeters (being Wall Streeters) often over-react to this figure, since experience has shown it most certainly will be "revised" later.

Flat Yield Curve: An infrequent condition when investors receive similar yields on bonds of similar credit risk at all maturity lengths. (See *Inverted Yield Curve* and *Yield Curve*.)

Flight to Quality: Movement of capital to higher quality securities during periods of market instability or uncertainty.

Floater: Slang for a floating-rate note; i.e., a security on which the interest rate is indexed to a money market instrument, such as six-month T-bills.

Float/Floating Supply: The amount of a company's stock available for immediate purchase.

Flower Bonds: Discounted U.S. government bonds that are valued at par for federal estate tax purposes when owned by the decedent at the time of death.

Foreign Exchange Risk: The risk associated with the translation of dollars into foreign currency, or vice versa, because of exchange rate fluctuations.

Formula Investing: Any "mechanical" approach to stock selection that emphasized a single variable, such as low P/E or high dividend yield.

Forward Contract: An agreement to deliver some commodity, security, or currency at a set price on some future date. Similiar in principle to a futures contract, except that forward contracts are not as liquid, buyers and sellers negotiate directly, and physical delivery is normally expected to take place.

Four Nines: Gold with a "fineness" of .9999, the purest possible.

Fourth Market: Direct trading of large blocks of securities between institutional investors that bypasses the various exchanges as well as the broker/dealer network.

Four Tigers: A term for the high-growth economies of Korea, Hong Kong, Singapore, and Taiwan. Also referred to as NICs (newly-industrialized countries).

Front-Running: An illegal practice, whereby a broker of trader takes advantage of a large incoming order—one that's sure to "move the market"—by executing an identical trade in his own account—first.

Fully Invested: A portfolio with minimal cash reserves.

Fundamentals: The "fundamentals" of a stock would include its price-earnings ratio (P/E), dividend yield, price-to-book value, earnings-per-share growth rate, etc.

Fungible: Identical, interchangeable assets. For example, a share of IBM stock has equal value to any other share of IBM stock and therefore can be substituted or delivered in its place.

Futures Option: A put or call option on a futures contract. Definitely not for the faint-of-heart.

Gap: Created when a stock's price range on a given day does not overlap the high and low prices of the previous day. When a gap initiates a trend (gapping up), it is called a "breakaway" or "runaway" gap; an "exhaustion" gap ends or reverses a trend.

Gilts: British Treasuries.

GNP Deflator: An important index used to inflation-adjust the prices of goods and services that comprise the Gross National Product, thereby enabling an analysis in constant dollars. The GNP deflator is a broadly based index and is often considered a better measure of inflation than the CPI or the PPI.

Golden Parachute: Lucrative payments that corporate executives receive in the event of a hostile takeover and their jobs are terminated.

Good Money: Slang for money that's available for immediate use, such as Fed funds.

Governments: Market jargon for government securities.

Greater Fool Theory: Facetiously states that regardless of how much an investor pays for a stock, there will always be another "investor" willing to pay an even higher price. The greater fool theory is most clearly in evidence during highly speculative markets.

Greenmail: An anti-takeover maneuver where the besieged corporation buys a raider's stock at a premium without offering other shareholders the same opportunity.

Group of Seven (G-7): The major industrial nations of the world—the U.S., Japan, West Germany, France, Great Britain, Canada, and Italy—whose finance ministers and central bankers meet periodically to discuss problems of mutual interest, such as dollar stabilization, etc.

Haircut: A discount.

Head and Shoulders Top: In technical analysis, a chart formation indicating a stock (or the market) is about to "take a bath."

Hedge: Any combination of offsetting long and/or short positions taken in order to reduce risk.

Hidden Assets: Assets which are significantly understated or do not appear on a corporation's balance sheet. Real estate purchased 40 years ago, for example, could appear at cost rather than at current market value.

Hit the Bid: When a trader accepts the highest price offered for a stock, he is said to have "hit the bid."

"Hot Seat": A special chair in a client service meeting reserved for a money manager whose performance has fallen into the bottom quartile.

Humble: What the stock market does to every investment manager on a regular basis!

Immunization: A form of "passive" fixed-income management. It refers to the design of a bond portfolio that blends maturities in such a way that the portfolio's target rate of return is "immunized" or protected against interest rate fluctuations. For example, if there is a rise in interest rates that reduces the portfolio value by 10%, that interest rate hike also reduces the amount of the liabilities by 10%, so assets and liabilities remain matched.

Implied Volatility: A term used in options trading that refers to the market's expectation of future price volatility, as implied by current option premiums. Shades of *Delta*!

"Information-less" Trading: Jargon for "passive investing" or indexing.

In Play: A company is said to be "in play" when its stock is rapidly moving up on high volume, and is widely perceived to be the target of a takeover attempt.

Insider: Technically, an insider is any director, officer, or owner of 10% or more of the equity of a corporation. By extension, the term may also include attorneys, accountants, investment bankers and others, including employees, who have access to privileged information.

Interbank Currency Market: A twenty-four-hour global market that exists to fill the growing need of business to hedge exchange risk in the face of rapidly fluctuating currency values.

Interest-Sensitive Stocks: Stocks in industries such as utilities that are highly responsive to changes in interest rates.

In the Money: An option that can be exercised at a profit; i.e., a call option whose *strike* or *exercise price* is below the price of the underlying stock, or a put option when the strike price is greater than the price of the underlying security. For example, a September $50 call option would be in the money if the stock was selling at $60 per share.

Inverted Yield Curve: An infrequent condition when short-term interest rates are higher than long-term rates. An inverted yield curve can result from Fed tightening near the end of a business cycle and is often a precursor of a slowing economy and, ultimately, a recession. Also referred to as *negative yield curve*.

Investment Banking: Mark Russell said it best: "Investment banking has become to productive enterprise in this country what mud wrestling is to the performing arts."

IPO: Shorthand for initial public offering.

January Effect: The historic pattern of equities, particularly those of smaller companies, to experience sharp price increases in January. This effect has been confirmed by academicians who attribute it to the reestablishment of positions at the start of a new year after tax-loss selling late in the previous year.

Jawboning: What the Fed does when "moral suasion" doesn't work.

Junk Bonds: Debt securities that have very high yields because they carry below-investment grade credit ratings (BB and below). Junk bonds, or *high yield bonds*, (as Drexel Burnham prefers to call them) are issued by companies without long credit histories or with questionable financial strength and have been a major source of financing for LBOs or hostile takeovers.

Kaffirs: Shares of South African gold producers.

Kondratieff Wave: What enthusiastic crowds often do at Russian sporting events.

Laddering: Spreading fixed-income securities evenly over a range of maturities.

LBO (Leveraged Buyout): Takeover of a company (either hostile or friendly) using borrowed funds. Generally, the target company's assets serve as security for the loans with the expectation that the debt will be repaid out of cash flow or from the sale of assets (*asset stripping*).

Leadership/Market Leadership: Stocks or industry groups that over time exhibit strong relative price advances on high trading volume. Many technical analysts believe that the "quality" of leadership often indicates future market trends.

Learning Curve: Hopefully what you have shortened by reading this book!

Liar: Bernard Baruch's term for anyone who claims to consistently buy at the bottom and sell at the top.

LIBOR (The London Interbank Offered Rate): The basic short-term rate of interest in Europe's financial markets; similar to the prime rate in the U.S.

Lifting A Leg: Closing out one side of a spread or hedged position.

Lighten Up: To sell part of a security position; to trim back a portfolio.

Limit Up, Limit Down: The maximum daily price change allowed by the commodity exchanges.

Liquidity: The ease with which an asset can be quickly bought or sold with a relatively small impact on prices. T-Bills are highly "liquid" while shares of small-cap stocks are often "illiquid." A portfolio is said to be liquid if it contains a large percentage of cash and easily marketable securities.

Long Hedge: Buying calls, selling puts or buying futures to protect against rising prices. *Short hedge:* selling calls, buying puts, or selling futures to protect against falling prices.

Long Position: An investor who buys a stock is said to have a "long position" or to be "long the security."

Long the Basis: Going long a commodity or security and selling a futures contract.

Market Inefficiency: The failure of the market to properly price a security, thereby creating an investment opportunity. Securities that are not widely followed by Wall Street analysts are most likely to be inefficiently priced.

Market Multiple: A term used to describe the price-earnings (P/E) ratio of the overall market. When the market multiple moves higher, it is referred to as a *multiple expansion*; when the market multiple moves lower, it is referred to as a *multiple contraction*.

Market Sector: A group of securities such as interest-sensitive stocks, consumer staples, or export-sensitive companies that share common investment characteristics. Investment professionals make a major sector bet when they "overweight" a particular sector in the belief it will outperform the overall market.

Market Sentiment: Refers to market "psychology" (bullish or bearish) as measured by various indicators, such as the put-to-call ratio, mutual fund cash positions, specialist short sales, and the number of investment advisory newsletters that are bullish or bearish. Technical analysts often view these sentiment readings as *contrary indicators*.

Market Tone: The "health" of the market in terms of trading activity and firmness of prices. Traders refer to a market as having a good (or positive) tone, or bad (or negative) tone.

Married Put: Buying a stock and simultaneously buying a put option on the stock.

Marry a Stock: Holding a stock long after its relative attractiveness has diminished.

Matrix Trading: A fancy term for bond swapping.

Mature Industry: An industry, such as tobacco, petroleum, or food, characterized by such slow growth that companies can expand only through gaining relative market share, by raising prices, or by diversifying.

Maximize Shareholder Value: When the board of directors of an undervalued company announces it will seek to "maximize shareholder value," it is signaling to investors its intention to seek a friendly suitor or that a *restructuring* is in the works.

Modern Portfolio Theory (MPT): The body of theory regarding the selection of optimal combinations of assets in a securities portfolio in order to produce the highest possible return for a given level of risk or the least possible risk for a given level of return. The emphasis is not on how securities will perform in isolation, but rather on how they will perform in combination. While much of MPT is regarded as academic rather than practical, its major tenet that reward is directly related to risk is widely accepted by investment practitioners.

Momentum Investing or Trend Following: An investment strategy based on the assumption that a trend, once established, will tend to continue.

Monetize the Debt: Said of the Federal Reserve when it increases the supply of money.

Moving Average: The average price of a stock calculated over specific time periods, typically 30, 60, 90, 100 or 200 days. A stock trading above its moving average is generally considered to be in an uptrend, while a stock trading below its moving average is generally considered to be in a downtrend.

Naked Option: A quick way to lose both your shirt and pants in the options market.

Net Free Reserves: Excess reserves less member bank borrowings at the Federal Reserve. When bank liquidity is rising, the Fed's monetary policy is generally thought to be "accommodative" or "expansionary."

"Net-Net": To a value investor, it doesn't get any better. To determine "net-net," deduct a company's current and long-term liabilities from current assets, and divide by the number of outstanding shares. If this number exceeds the price of the stock, the investor, in effect, gets the underlying business and any earnings for free.

Nickel/Dime: Trader's slang for a bond's movement, up or down, of five/ten basis points. Example: "Bonds were up a nickel today."

Nikkei: Japan's major market index, consisting of 225 stocks.

Nominal Return: The rate of return on an investment without any adjustment for inflation.

Noncallable: A bond that cannot be redeemed by the issuer prior to maturity or a specified period. Such a bond is said to have *call protection*.

"Non-Fundamental" Trading: Wall Street jargon for indexing.

Normalized Earnings: Earnings that have been adjusted for cyclical variations.

Novation: Substituting or replacing new debt for old debt.

Off-Board: Over-the-counter transactions, particularly in stocks listed on one of the major exchanges.

On the Sidelines: Said of a money manager who has turned neutral or negative toward the market, has "raised some cash," and is now "sitting on the sidelines."

Open Market Operations: The Federal Reserve's primary policy tool. All its activities (the buying and selling of Treasury securities in the secondary market) that influence the supply of money and the level of interest rates.

OPM: The lifeblood of Wall Street—Other People's Money.

Ordinary Shares: British term for common stocks.

Out of the Money: In the jargon of an option specialist, an option with "time value but no intrinsic value." To the rest of us, the term refers to a call option whose strike or exercise price is above the price of the underlying stock. A put option is "out of the money" when the strike price is less than the price of the underlying security. For example, a September $50 call option would be out of the money if the stock was selling at $40 per share.

Overbought: A technical condition when a security or market has risen quickly and dramatically and is thus vulnerable to a correction. Similarly, a security or market may be oversold and due for a rally if it has experienced a rapid and sharp decline.

Overhang/Overhanging Supply: A large block of stock, either on the market or soon to be on the market, that puts downward pressure on the price of a security. For example, an overhang could be created by a secondary offering in registration or by an institutional holder attempting to sell a large position.

Overvalued: Refers to a security or market trading at a higher price than can be justified on a fundamental basis. An *undervalued* security or market trades at a discount to its fair market value. A *fairly valued* security or market trades at a reasonable price given its fundamentals, while a *fully valued* security or market trades at or near the maximum price justified by its fundamentals.

Package Trading: Euphemism for program trading (the "P" word).

Paper: Slang for relatively short-term debt securities.

Pass-Through: Mortgage-backed securities (such as Ginnie Maes—obligations of the Government National Mortgage Association) are a hybrid debt instrument that represent an undivided interest in a pool of mortgages and which "pass through" to investors payments of both principal and interest from the underlying mortgages (after deduction of a service fee).

Paying-Up: Said of an investor who pays a "rich" or premium price for a stock after failing to purchase it at a lower price because he is more concerned about "missing" the stock than about overpaying for it.

Phantom Income: Income that's taxed, even though it's not received; for example, the interest "accreted" on a zero coupon bond.

Pickup: The gain in yield (usually expressed in basis points) from a bond swap.

Picture: When a portfolio manager asks his trader for a "picture" on GE, he's looking for more than just a quote & "size" (the number of shares available); he also wants to find out: "What's around? Who's been active in the stock?"

Plain Vanilla: Jargon to describe a securities issue without any "come-on" features such as calls, puts or warrants (these features are often referred to as "bells and whistles").

Point: For stocks, a point is one dollar; in the case of bonds a point means $10.00, since a bond is quoted as a percentage of $1,000 (par). Thus, a bond that gains 3 points has appreciated $30.00 in value.

Poison Pill: Any of a variety of anti-takeover defense strategies triggered when control of a corporation is threatened by a hostile raider. Often used interchangeably with *shark repellent*.

Poison-Puts: Developed in reaction to the near-disastrous impact of the RJR-Nabisco deal on corporate bond holders. Poison-puts give bondholders the option of selling their bonds back to the issuer at par in case of a hostile takeover or if the issuer's credit rating is downgraded as a result of a friendly merger or LBO.

Pork Bellys in Pinstripes: Slang for financial futures.

Portfolio Insurance: P.T. Barnum would have loved it! A controversial, and now discredited, portfolio hedging technique enthusiastically endorsed by institutional investors (before October 1987) that includes the use of financial futures in an attempt to protect equity portfolios against market declines. Also called *dynamic hedging*.

Private Market Value: Despite the strong bull market of the 1980s, many public companies today are still selling below the cost of replacing their assets or what those assets would bring if sold off. These "discounts" will continue to attract corporate buyers who are more interested in the "private market value" of a company than on overall stock market or economic trends.

Privatization: The opposite of *nationalization*. When a government returns to the private sector state-controlled businesses or industries.

Producer Price Index (PPI): An index of price changes at the wholesale level.

Profit-Taking: A euphemism for, "I have no idea why the market (or a particular stock) was down yesterday."

Program Trading: Refers to a variety of computer-driven trading strategies involving the simultaneous purchase or sale of 15 or more stocks. The most controversial of these is *stock-index arbitrage*, in which traders buy or sell "baskets" of stocks with offsetting trades in stock-index futures or stock-index options to lock in price differences between the two markets. (If stocks are temporarily "cheaper" than futures, for example, arbitragers will buy stocks and sell futures.) It's the most controversial form of program trading because it can accelerate market moves, if not actually cause them. Critics of stock-index arbitrage argue that the activity is a destabilizing influence on the market since it can result in the NYSE being bombarded with sell orders in a matter of minutes.

"Pull the Plug": To sell a stock at a loss to avoid an even bigger loss.

Pure Play: Investments concentrated in securities that provide maximum exposure to a particular investment theme. An investor seeking a "perestroika play" might purchase Pepsico or Occidental Petroleum, two U.S. companies that stand to benefit from the political and economic liberalization of the Eastern bloc. However, a "pure" perestroika play would be to buy a *country fund*, such as the Germany Fund or the Hungarian Fund.

Quality of Earnings: Because of accounting gimmickry, many security analysts believe that the "quality of earnings" has declined in recent years. As a result, they argue that "true operating profits" are a more accurate gauge of a company's financial health than "reported earnings," which can easily be manipulated.

Quantitative Analysis: Investment analysis that focuses on quantitative or measurable factors such as asset value, revenues, profitability, financial ratios, etc., as opposed to qualitative considerations such as competence of management, product quality, or strategic positioning. The person who performs this type of analysis is referred to as a *quant*, or "rocket scientist." At an early age, most quants were likely known as "nerds."

Random-Walk Theory: The hypothesis that since security price changes are "serially independent," an investor can do as well buying stocks at random (throwing darts at the stock table of the *Wall Street Journal*) as he can using fundamental or technical analysis. Naturally, professional investment managers vigorously dispute this argument.

Rate Anticipation Swap: The sale of a bond of one maturity and the simultaneous purchase of a bond of different maturity to take advantage of an expected change in interest rates.

Ratio Analysis: Various types of measures used to gauge the financial health of a company. Ratio analysis is often used by security analysts to compare companies within a particular industry. Examples of financial ratios include return on equity, return on assets, current ratio, debt/equity ratio and inventory-to-sales-ratio.

Real Estate Investment Trust (REIT): A publicly-traded investment security that purchases and manages real estate and/or real estate loan portfolios. Historically, REITs have attracted investors because of their high yields.

Real Rate of Return: A return adjusted for inflation. For example, an investor earning 8% on a certificate of deposit during a period of 5% inflation is receiving a real rate of return of 3%.

Regression Analysis: Investment management consultants love to toss this term around! Essentially it involves the mindless number-crunching of a money manager's track record in order to rationalize a "guesstimate" as to how well (poorly) he will perform in the future.

Relative Strength: How a stock/industry/market sector performs relative to the overall market. For example, if a stock appreciated 10% while the overall market rises 20%, market technicians refer to the stock as having poor relative strength.

Relative Value: The attractiveness of one security compared to another in terms of risk, liquidity and expected return.

Reorganization: A head-to-toe restructuring of a company's financial position, usually under duress; often results in creditors receiving new securities in exchange for old in an attempt to keep the company afloat.

Repurchase Agreement (REPO): Essentially a sale-repurchase agreement; a loan secured by collateral in the form of governments. In financial lingo, a U.S. government securities dealer will say he is going to "repo securities." On the other hand, a money market fund will "do repos."

Reverse Hedge: Going long a call and shorting the underlying security.

Riding the Yield Curve: A strategy whereby an investor gains an incremental return by extending bond maturities to benefit from a positive yield curve.

Risk Arbitrage: Risk arbitrageurs (ARBS) try to profit from takeover activity by assuming long positions in the target firm's stock (and sometimes shorting the acquiring firm's stock). The risk, of course, is that the buyout will be unsuccessful. Risk arbitrage differs from *riskless arbitrage*, which entails "locking in" or profiting from price differentials on essentially identical securities.

Risk-Free Return: A theoretical return, earned with "perfect certainty;" i.e., without risk: approximated by the yield on 90-day T-bills.

Round Trip: When a money manager rides a stock up, fails to sell it, then rides it back down again.

Rule of 72: A rule of thumb on how long it takes to double your money: simply divide the number 72 by the rate of return or yield. Thus an investor earning 15% per year will double his money in roughly 4.8 years.

Samurai Bond: A yen-denominated bond issued in Japan by non-Japanese entities.

Secondary Stocks: Stocks of smaller companies generally traded over-the-counter or on the AMEX. Secondary stocks have smaller capitalizations, tend to be more volatile, and are usually purchased for price appreciation rather than dividend yield.

Secular Trend: A relatively long-term trend as contrasted to a cyclical trend.

Securitization: The packaging of financial transactions, such as bank loans (asset-backed securities or ABS) or a pool of mortgages (mortgage-backed securities or MBS), into tradeable securities.

Selling Off/Sell Off: Said of the market when it experiences a "hiccup."

Selling Short: Selling borrowed stock to take advantage of an anticipated drop in the stock's price. An investor who sells a stock short is said to have a "short position" or to be "short" the security.

Sell Side: Retail and institutional brokers and traders who transact orders comprise Wall Street's sell side. Banks, insurance companies, mutual funds, independent investment managers and other institutional investors who originate and place orders make up the *buy side*.

Shogun Bond: Generally refers to a dollar-denominated bond issued in Japan by a U.S. corporation and sold to Japanese investors.

Short Squeeze: The pressure that can build on short sellers to cover (buy back) their positions and replace borrowed shares as the price of a shorted stock soars. *Short interest* refers to the number of shares of a particular stock that have been sold short, but have not yet been repurchased.

Singles and Doubles: What conservative money managers try to "hit"; aggressive managers prefer to "swing for the bleachers" in hopes of hitting a "home run."

Smokestack Stocks: Companies often located in the "rustbelt" that are involved in basic manufacturing—auto, steel, aluminum, rubber, etc.

Snugging: Mild "tightening" by the Fed.

Socially Responsible Investing: An investment philosophy that emphasizes the purchase of companies whose products or activities are socially acceptable or morally responsible. Ethical investors often avoid companies with operations in South Africa, with records of environmental abuse, with defense-related businesses or such *sin stocks* as tobaccos and liquors.

Soft Dollars: Payment for value-added services through commissions generated from security trades, as opposed to *hard dollar,* or cash payment.

South: Slang for declining prices—"Stocks are headed south."

Sovereign or Country Risk: The risk associated with investing in a foreign country, such as nationalization of private business, repudiation of debt, etc.

Special Situation: A stock that an analyst believes should rise in value in the near future because of anticipated favorable developments. *Turkeys:* What many special situations turn out to be.

Spike: A sudden sharp rise in the price of a stock followed by just as sudden a fall.

Spread: When buying or selling a security, spread refers to the difference between the bid and asked price. Generally, the more illiquid a security, the larger the spread.

Staggering Maturities: Hedging a fixed-income portfolio against interest rate risk by buying bonds with a range of maturities.

Standard Error of Independent Return (SEIR): Except for the faculty at Wharton Business School and a handful of "number crunchers" at SEI, no one really knows or cares what this term means.

Sticky Deal: A new underwriting that's not going well.

Stock-Index Futures: Contracts to buy or sell the cash value of a stock index by a certain date. Stock-index futures can be used to speculate on the future direction of the market or to hedge a portfolio against a market decline. Created in 1982, today trading in stock-index futures rivals that of the stocks themselves. Critics argue that these futures contribute to stock market volatility; defenders say they make markets more efficient and provide ways to reduce risk.

Stock-Index Option: An option based on an underlying stock index—such as the S&P 500—rather than an individual security.

Stock Screen: A computer-aided method of selecting stocks by screening a large universe of securities based on predetermined criteria such as low P/E, high dividend yield, low price to book, or rapid earnings growth.

Stop-Loss Order: A stop-loss order is designed to limit losses or protect gains on a position already held. An investor with a stop-loss order has his position sold or *stopped out* when the security trades at his specified price or below.

Story Stock: A security that goes up in price because of a "sexy story," and not necessarily on the basis of its fundamental value.

Straits Times Index: The Singapore Exchange's equivalent of the S&P 500.

Strategic Buyers: Rapidly becoming the dominant players in the takeover game as high stock prices, political hostility, and legal and financial considerations have made it more difficult and expensive for swashbucklers to launch successful raids. In a *strategic merger*, the acquiring company is motivated more by how the two companies can fit together long-term (the "synergy" they can create) than by how quickly they can strip the assets or milk the cash flow.

Street: Short for Wall Street, the major artery in New York City's financial district. By extension it refers to the financial community at large.

Strips: An acronyn for Separate Trading of Registered Interest & Principal of Securities. A "zero-coupon bond" issued directly by the Treasury. A genuine "no-brainer" to a hold-to-maturity investor.

Strips, Straps, Straddles and Spreads: Trading strategies in the options and commodities markets.

Stub Stocks: Stubs represent the small amount of equity that remains at companies that have undergone a *leveraged recapitalization* or have become privately controlled in a leveraged buyout. Highly volatile, stub stocks may trade on the New York or other exchanges and are considered quite speculative.

Swaption: Just-when-you-thought-you-had-heard-it-all; a "swaption" refers to an option on an interest-rate swap.

Swissy: Slang for Swiss francs.

Synthetic Position: A position that produces the same results as if another position were held. For example, buying a call and selling a put on the same stock is the equivalent of owning the underlying security and is therefore called a synthetic position.

Taking A View: British term for "forecasting."

Technical Analysis: Technical analysts study such market indicators as the advance/decline index, on-balance volume, the high-low index, and relative strength to gain insight into overall market trends and to help detect shifts in supply and demand for individual stocks. It should be noted that many fundamental analysts view technical analysis with the same skepticism as they view astrology or palm reading.

TED Spread: The spread between T-bills & Eurodollar CDs (LIBOR).

Theme Investing: Some "top-down" managers seek to identify and exploit investment themes such as disinflation or the reindustrialization of America by overweighting their portfolios with stocks expected to benefit from these trends.

Theta, Lambda, Kappa, Gamma, Rho: A kind of co-ed sorority or fraternity limited to students working toward an advanced degree in options trading.

Thin Market: A market for a security characterized by low trading volume and large spreads between bids and offers, thereby making it difficult to buy or sell large blocks of stock without significantly affecting the price.

Tight Market: A market characterized by heavy volume and narrow spreads between bid and asked prices.

Tom Next: Short for "tomorrow next." Refers to a transaction on the foreign-exchange market that will be settled on the next business day.

Ton: Bond trader's jargon for $100 million.

Topping Out: A security or market that has risen significantly and is now starting to level out and decline. Another common expression is that the market "looks toppy."

Trading Range: The high and low prices between which a security or the overall market has been, or is expected to be, trading; at the bottom of the range the security or market is said to have *support*, while at the top it encounters *resistance*. A *break-out* or *break-down* occurs when a stock or market penetrates the resistance area or breaks below the support area.

Tranche: A collateralized mortgage obligation (CMO) is a debt security backed by a pool of mortgages divided into separate issues of differing maturities with each issue called a tranche.

Treasuries: Debt obligations (I.O.U.s) issued by the Treasury and backed by the U.S. government. *Agencies* are debt instruments issued by federal agencies, but technically are not a direct obligation of the U.S. government.

Treasury Bill Auction: The auction by the U.S. Treasury in which short-term (usually three-month, six-month or one-year) debt obligations are offered on a discount basis. T-bills pay no interest, but mature at full face value.

Trendline: A straight line (or parallel lines) drawn on a chart connecting the lowest and highest points of a price movement that indicates to market technicians the direction a particular stock or market index is trending.

Triple Witching Hour: The last trading hour on the third Friday of March, June, September, and December, when options and futures on stock indexes and options on individual stocks expire concurrently, sometimes setting off frenzied activity as traders and arbitragers unwind their positions.

Trustee: A person or institution such as a bank trust department that manages assets for the benefit of a third party; not to be confused with "trusty."

Turnaround: A security that has fallen substantially in price due to deteriorating fundamentals and which may attract "contrarians or bottom fishers" who believe that the worst is over and that better times lie ahead.

Uncertainty: The one sure thing in the stock market.

Unched (pronounced unch'd): If a stock is neither up nor down for the day, but "unchanged" from the previous day's close, brokers jocularly refer to it as being "unched."

Underlier: The security or other asset on which an option is written.

Unwind: To reverse, close out or liquidate an investment position.

Value Investing: A philosophy of investing pioneered by Benjamin Graham and David Dodd that emphasizes the purchase of stocks below their *intrinsic value* in the belief that patient investors will eventually be rewarded ("value will out"). To a Graham and Dodd disciple, net asset value is more important than projected earnings.

Wall Street Economist: A paid guesser.

Whipsawed: Said of a money manager who has consistently been on the "wrong side" of a volatile market (zigging when he should have been zagging and vice versa).

Whisper Stock: A stock that is on the "whisper circuit"—i.e., is the subject of takeover rumors.

White Knight: A corporation or investor group that buys, on a friendly basis, a company that is the target of a hostile takeover.

Widow-and-Orphan Stock: A relatively safe and high-yielding stock thought to be suitable for even the most risk-averse investor.

Window Dressing: End-of-quarter trading activity (selling "losers" and buying "winners") designed to "dress up" a portfolio to give clients the impression they have been in the right stocks.

Yankee Bond: A dollar-denominated bond sold in the U.S. by a foreign entity.

Yield: The annual return on a security from dividends or interest. There are many ways to calculate yield—dividend yield, coupon yield, current yield, yield to maturity, yield to call and yield to average life.

Yield Curve: Represents the difference between yields on short-term and long-term government bonds. The yield curve will normally be "upward sloping" (positive yield curve), meaning the yields on long-term bonds exceed those on short-term bonds to compensate investors for the extra risk they are taking.

Yield Rally: Wall Street euphemism for a sharp drop in bond prices.

Yield Spread: The difference in yield between various securities. Yield spread may be caused by various factors, including maturity length, quality ratings, etc.

Zerial: Slang for a "serial" zero-coupon bond.

Zero Coupon Bond: A debt security that has been "stripped" of its coupons and, therefore, does not pay any interest prior to maturity. Zero coupon bonds generally trade at substantial discounts from face value, and are the most volatile of all fixed-income securities. Zeros have the advantage of eliminating *reinvestment risk*; i.e., the yield to maturity is locked in at time of purchase.

Zero Sum Game: For someone to win, someone else has to lose.

INDEX

I

S

T

U

V